fast track»

ROBERT'S RULES OF ORDER

JIM SLAUGHTER

Penguin Random House

Publisher Mike Sanders
Acquisitions Editor Brandon Buechley
Development Editor Jan Lynn Neal
Copy Editor Rick Kughen
Art Director William Thomas
Cover Designer Jessica Lee
Book Designer/Layout Ayanna Lacey
Indexer Celia McCoy
Proofreader Lisa Himes

First American Edition, 2022
Published in the United States by DK Publishing
6081 E. 82nd Street, Indianapolis, IN 46250

Published in the United States by Dorling Kindersley Limited.

Library of Congress Catalog Number: 2022931019
ISBN: 978-0-74405-697-6

DK books are available at special discounts when purchased
in bulk for sales promotions, premiums, fundraising,
or educational use. For details, contact:
SpecialSales@dk.com

Printed in China

For the curious
www.dk.com

Contents

Introduction

You can improve your organization through the proper use of parliamentary procedure. Your meetings will be shorter as well as fairer. Your organization's decisions will be defensible, both as to process and legality. With that said, there's a lot to parliamentary procedure. The newest *Robert's Rules of Order Newly Revised* is 714 pages. While that might seem shorter than the prior edition, there are more words on each page!

This *Fast-Track* guide is not *Robert's*. It's not an exhaustive treatise on every motion you can make at a meeting (or we would have called it the *Excruciatingly Painful Slow-Start Guide*). Instead, the book you hold is designed to get you up and running for your next meeting as quickly as possible. In other words, it puts you on the fast track to mastering the basics of parliamentary procedure.

Much of *Robert's* is designed for large membership meetings or conventions. But there are many other types of meetings:

- Condominium and homeowners association (also known as community associations) board meetings
- Church and religious organization meetings
- School board, city council, and county commission meetings
- Nonprofit board of directors meetings

These are just a few of the many kinds of meetings that can benefit from proper parliamentary procedure. This book identifies what procedures are best suited for large assemblies and when relaxed procedures may be appropriate for a committee or smaller board.

How This Book Is Organized

Although you should feel free to turn to whatever chapter interests you most, I encourage you to read the first two chapters before moving forward. **Chapters 1 and 2** examine fundamental concepts that are necessary to use parliamentary procedure. Tempted to skip these chapters? Don't!

Chapters 3, 4, 5, and 6 explore what most people consider to be true parliamentary procedure. That is, how business is brought before an assembly and the motions used to perfect or defeat such items of business. Closely related is **Chapter 7,** which examines the purpose and practice of voting at meetings.

Chapter 8 looks at the officers in organizations, their duties, and the election process.

The final chapters deal with meetings, including how to plan, run, and document good meetings. **Chapter 9** details the types of business meetings and what can and can't be done at each. **Chapter 10** is focused on the requirements for (as well as tips for) holding successful electronic meetings. **Chapter 11** provides suggestions on organizing meetings for maximum efficiency. **Chapter 12** discusses how best to record what happened at your meeting. Finally, **Chapter 13** provides suggestions for avoiding or repairing meeting problems, both before and during your meetings.

Beyond these chapters, this Fast-Track guide provides useful information in other ways. Appendix A gives resources for learning more about procedure, including parliamentary organizations, books, and websites. Appendix B is a guide to frequently used parliamentary motions from *Robert's Rules of Order Newly Revised (12th Edition)*.

Acknowledgments

My interest in parliamentary procedure was nurtured and has been maintained by a number of excellent parliamentarians, many of whom are now gone. Mentioning specific names is always risky (because someone will inevitably be left out), but I must express my appreciation to three outstanding parliamentary colleagues and friends, Jon Ericson, Gaut Ragsdale, and Nancy Sylvester.

My first experience with parliamentary procedure might be like yours. As a youth, I went to a meeting and was run over by other members who knew more about procedure than I did. Hearing my complaint, my parents gave me a book on parliamentary procedure, so I could figure out what happened.

Robert's Rules of Order: Fast-Track—The Brief and Easy Guide to Parliamentary Procedure was reviewed by two parliamentary attorneys from my law firm who double-checked the accuracy of what you'll learn here and ensure that this book gives you everything you need to know about parliamentary procedure. Special thanks are extended to Carole Albright and Michael Taliercio.

More appreciation than I can express goes to my wife, Tamara, and my three (now grown) sons Freeman, McKinley, and Wyatt. They have encouraged me and put up with my long hours and crazy work travel for much of their lives.

Trademarks

All terms mentioned in this book that are known to be or are suspected of being trademarks or service marks have been appropriately capitalized. Alpha Books and Penguin Group (USA) Inc. cannot attest to the accuracy of this information. Use of a term in this book should not be regarded as affecting the validity of any trademark or service mark.

Chapter 1

What Is Parliamentary Procedure?

Because you picked up this book (and are still holding it), you must have some interest in meeting procedures. Even so, it might help to start with some explanation. The term *parliamentary procedure* is likely broader than you think. That's because the phrase encompasses everything that goes into running a legal and effective meeting, including these procedures:

- Giving proper notice of the meeting to members
- Waiting until enough members show up before starting the meeting
- Discussing and voting on issues at the meeting

All these considerations and more fall under the heading *parliamentary procedure.*

If you attend business meetings, you should at least learn the basics of parliamentary procedure. For one thing, state laws and association governing documents often prescribe the rules organizations must follow to transact business. As a result, ignoring or incorrectly applying parliamentary procedure can lead to embarrassment, hard feelings, and even lawsuits. But the benefits of a well-run meeting go far beyond legal concerns. Proper procedure can turn long, confrontational meetings into short, painless ones. If you're a leader, that's a good way to keep members happy.

What Parliamentary Procedure Is Not

It's almost easier to discuss what parliamentary procedure is *not*, rather than what it *is*. Parliamentary procedure is not just a book called *Robert's Rules of Order*. *Robert's* is the best-known book on parliamentary procedure, but there are others. Depending on your specific group, *Robert's* might not even be relevant. For instance, organizations of physicians and dentists often use some version of a book entitled *The Standard Code of Parliamentary Procedure* as their guide to meetings. State legislatures often fall back on *Mason's Manual of Legislative Procedure*. Such groups don't talk about or refer to *Robert's Rules of Order*. It's just not their book.

With that said, I spend much of this book discussing *Robert's*. That's because, without question, it's the 800-pound gorilla of the parliamentary world.

A *parliamentary authority* is a book on meeting procedure that is followed because of an adopted rule or bylaws language. Among organizations with a *parliamentary authority*, most use (or at least claim to use) *Robert's*.

Robert's Rules and parliamentary procedure are viewed as one and the same by most of the public. Some courts have held that *Robert's* can be relied upon even without a required parliamentary book. The fact that *Robert's* is the most popular and easiest-to-locate book on parliamentary procedure argues strongly in its favor as a parliamentary authority.

Parliamentary procedure isn't just about motions either, such as the motion to Adjourn or for the Previous Question. Sure, motions are how business is transacted in a formal meeting. But motions only take up about a third of the current *Robert's*. The rest of the book is a wonderful resource for anyone who has to spend time in meetings.

For instance, there's a chapter on how to run a meeting if you've never presided over one before (aptly named "Suggestions for Inexperienced Presiding Officers"). One chapter describes how to take minutes, noting that you don't need to write down what people say, just what was done (see Chapter 12). There's even a set of sample minutes. Another chapter explores options for dealing with problem members or guests. A final chapter discusses how to remove an elected officer (if you're an officer, take comfort in knowing that hardly anyone ever reads that far in the book).

With all this discussion about what a great book *Robert's* is, let's talk for a moment on how to find the right book. Wait … find the right book? How hard can that be? Well, it's actually pretty confusing. The term "Robert's Rules" isn't copyrighted, so you'll find all sorts of books with the phrase "Robert's Rules" in the title. Big books. Little books. Books with cartoons. Even books that have nothing to do with parliamentary procedure! Most often, these other books are earlier editions of *Robert's* or knockoffs. While some are fine works, they likely aren't the one you're looking for, so you can end up with the wrong book by mistake.

There is always one official *Robert's* that is the successor to earlier works; the current edition is *Robert's Rules of Order Newly Revised (12th Edition)*. If your organization's rules specify the "latest edition" of *Robert's*, this is your book. The newest *Robert's* came out in late 2020 and can be identified by "12th Edition" on its cover and the fact that it's 714 pages long (without a single cartoon).

What Rules Should You Follow?

You might think the question of what rules should be followed in your organization would be fairly complicated, but it's not. There's a very specific legal answer: It depends. (Surely you've dealt with attorneys before.) The reason it depends is because different groups use different levels of procedure. While it can sometimes be more complicated, the general rule is that larger groups use more formal procedures, while smaller groups use less-formal procedures.

These levels of formality make sense. For instance, I serve as parliamentarian at several conventions that meet with thousands of delegates attending each year. In an effort to be fair, the rules of large conventions tend to be very formal. No delegate speaks without first being recognized by the chair. In fact, the floor microphone isn't even turned on until the member is given permission to speak. Once a delegate starts to speak, they have two minutes under the convention rules. At the end of two minutes, the microphone is turned off. No one speaks a second time as long as anyone who has not yet spoken wishes to speak a first time. While such rules might seem strict, they are necessary to be fair. After all, you can't easily have a conversation with a thousand people.

On the other hand, how formal do you want to be in your small board or committee? Boards often have only four or five members. A committee can be as small as one person. How formal do you want to be in your committee of one? ("I move to take a 10-minute bathroom break." "Oh, no, there's no one to second my motion!")

The same formality that helps a larger organization function can actually hinder a smaller body. With that in mind, *Robert's* and other parliamentary books recognize that committees and small boards should operate under more relaxed rules of procedure. Can such a committee or small board sometimes choose to operate more formally? Absolutely! If informality is preventing work from getting accomplished, a smaller group might choose to operate more formally with motions, seconds, and votes. For example, city councils, county commissions, and school boards tend to be more formal, even though they only have a few members. Such groups have decided that the importance of the issues they are addressing or the potential controversy with anything they do warrants dotting all i's and crossing all t's.

Different Procedures for Different Types of Groups

When it comes to procedure, business meetings don't need to be more formal than necessary to quickly and fairly transact business. However, that means the level of formality can vary depending on the size, nature, and the purpose of the group.

In the following sections, I describe some of the most common types of organizations and the procedures they typically follow.

Membership Meetings

Most organized societies have regular meetings of their members. This includes monthly meetings of nonprofits, regular union meetings, or the annual meeting of a condominium or homeowners association. At these meetings, any member can show up, and the group, by voting, can speak or act on behalf of the entire organization.

Typically, because of their larger size, membership meetings must be run fairly formally. Informal discussion of matters is impractical due to the number of members present. Limits on debate must be observed to keep the meeting on time. Formal votes help to avoid legal challenges. However, the latest edition of *Robert's* recognizes that such formal procedures might not be appropriate for membership meetings of small associations and recommends that a society with a dozen or fewer members consider adopting less formal rules to govern meetings.

Boards

Boards are typically smaller elected or appointed bodies with administrative or managerial duties. For instance, governmental boards are most often created and defined by statute or local ordinance. Typically, nonprofit association boards are defined in the governing documents of the organization. In all such instances, the board has such authority as is given to it. Boards sometimes go by slightly different names, which can include *boards of directors*, *boards of trustees*, or *executive boards*.

Because boards tend to be smaller, their procedure can be less formal. Just as a large group might find that proceeding informally causes confusion, a small board that attempts to be too formal might actually hinder business. As a consequence, *Robert's* provides that the rules governing a board meeting "where there are not more than about a dozen members present" is different in the following respects:

- Members may raise a hand instead of standing when seeking to obtain the floor.

- Members may remain seated while speaking or making motions.

- Motions need no second.

- Discussion of a subject is permitted while no motion is pending.

- When a proposal is clear, a vote can be taken without a formal motion.

- There is no limit to the number of times a member may speak to a subject or motion.

- Occasions in which debate must be limited or stopped should be rarer than in larger meetings.

- The chair is typically a full participant and can debate and vote on all questions.

- Votes are often taken by a show of hands.

Are all of these informal rules perfect for any board? No—yet once again, *Robert's* notes that smaller boards may choose to adopt more formal procedures given their circumstances.

Occasionally, you will see very large boards. For instance, a number of trade associations have boards in excess of 100 members. In these cases, the informal rules recommended by *Robert's* don't apply, and the group should operate much like a large membership meeting.

Conventions

Conventions are yearly (or even less frequent) gatherings of delegates who represent other members. For instance, a state or national association or union might have an annual convention to consider resolutions on behalf of the organization and vote on other important issues. Delegates to the convention may have one vote or may carry the many votes of the members they represent.

As you can imagine, the large size of a convention often requires even more strict rules than those found in *Robert's*. After all, 8,000 delegates (there are such meetings!) who all want to speak to an issue is impractical regardless of how long the convention lasts. Because of this, conventions frequently adopt supplemental rules that address issues of how long delegates can speak, how often delegates can speak, and even which motions can be made.

Committees

Committees tend to be small groups appointed to investigate or examine a specific issue and then report back to the larger body. In *Robert's*, a committee is different than the groups discussed earlier in that a committee has no independent authority. That is, such a group can't do anything by itself. If a committee wishes to do something other than what it was assigned, it must go back to the parent body and ask permission. Because committees are tasked with thoroughly discussing an issue, motions to close or limit debate are generally not permitted. Unless a committee is given different rules, most committees of any size tend to operate informally, like a small board.

Electronic Meetings

Given how our world has changed because of COVID-19, a new Chapter 10 about electronic meetings has been added to this book. Keep in mind, though, that in *Robert's*, a fundamental aspect of a meeting is "simultaneous aural communication." That is, everyone must be able to hear everybody else. *Robert's* does not recognize email, texting, or chat room discussions as meetings unless clearly authorized by the governing documents or state statute.

The Importance of Being Flexible

Are the various groups stuck with the types of procedures just described? Absolutely not! In fact, if you take nothing else from this book, you should understand that rules exist for the benefit of the group and not the other way around. Apply the Goldilocks rule: The meeting procedure should be "just right" for the particular assembly based on its size and the work to be accomplished.

Organizations should follow (or adopt) meeting procedures that help them accomplish their task (see the section "Special Rules of Order" in Chapter 2). To paraphrase what attorney Clarence Darrow said about laws, meeting procedures should be like clothes—they should be made to fit the organizations they serve.

Parliamentary procedure encompasses everything that goes into running effective and legal meetings. Learning the basics is a worthwhile endeavor. Not all meeting procedure is the same—different types of groups should use different levels of formality. The specific procedures should fit the assembly, not the other way around.

Chapter 2

Governing Documents and Parliamentary Procedure

You may be tempted to skip this chapter on governing documents and jump straight to the chapter on motions. Don't do it! While you might learn how motions are used to transact business in meetings, you first need to make sure that the information applies to *your* organization's meetings.

Higher Authorities Than *Robert's*

Higher written authorities, such as state or federal law or an organization's governing documents, can modify or completely override the language in a parliamentary authority. Sometimes these documents simply state which parliamentary book must be followed (which is important to know, so you don't end up using the wrong manual). Other times, though, statutes or governing documents detail the procedures to be followed in specific situations. If that's the case, the language in *Robert's* or another parliamentary book doesn't really matter. Statutes or governing authorities can modify or completely override the usual parliamentary practice.

These higher rules can be found in several places, and their importance is ranked. Higher documents in the hierarchy overrule lower documents. In addition, the consequences of violating different level documents can vary. A small violation of a lower-level document might not be that big of a deal after the fact. On the other hand, a violation of higher-level governing authority may be disastrous and have consequences long after a meeting.

The most common governing documents, ranked from most to least important, are as follows:

- Laws and statutes (most often at the state level)
- Corporate articles
- Bylaws
- Special rules of order
- Parliamentary authority

Because these documents are so important and can impact the parliamentary procedure in your organization, let's take a look at each.

Laws and Statutes

Now, wait a minute! Why is a book on parliamentary procedure suddenly talking about laws and statutes? Well, in today's world, that's where certain procedures are mandated for various organizations. For instance, federal laws govern labor unions and at times provide specific regulations on union voting and elections. State statutes impact city councils, school boards, county commissions, legislative bodies, and community associations (homeowners and condominium associations). Even nonprofit corporations—which include many volunteer associations—might be governed by state nonprofit statutes.

As is usually the case with the law, if a federal or state statute specifically addresses a meeting issue, you're done. You don't need to look any further. The statute wins. For example, a number of state laws provide that homeowners and condominium association meetings must be conducted "in accordance with the most recent edition of *Robert's Rules of Order Newly Revised*." With such language, you don't need to worry about what another book on procedure says. You couldn't adopt a different parliamentary authority even if you want to (unless the statute allows for such a change).

Other procedural statutes may give specific and very detailed provisions on the meeting process. For instance, governmental bodies (legislatures, city councils, county commissions, and school boards) are often governed by *sunshine laws*. Such laws usually require a certain amount or type of notice of meetings (and even motions) and prohibit certain actions except in open sessions. As a result, unlike private associations that can restrict meetings to members at any time, governmental bodies are generally prohibited from closing their meetings except in certain circumstances. Even then, the organization likely can't vote in closed sessions. Such specific procedural statutes override any language in the organization's bylaws or *Robert's*. To be unaware of such statutory language could lead to the wrong parliamentary answer and an embarrassing situation.

Even nonprofit associations—which include most organizations these days—are not safe from statutory involvement. More and more nonprofit procedures are governed by legislation. Thankfully, though, most (but not all) nonprofit statutes are a fallback to use if an organization's bylaws are silent on an issue. However, some new statutes governing nonprofits include mandatory provisions on what notice must be given for meetings; how many members must be present to hold a meeting; voting requirements for certain issues; what rules must be followed in meetings in certain instances; and, more recently, details on holding electronic (or *virtual*) meetings or making decisions without a meeting through electronic voting.

To get it all right, do you need a lawyer to accompany you to all meetings? No, of course not. Most meeting issues don't involve the concerns listed previously or rise to a level where it matters. And if they do, the good thing about these specific organizations (governmental bodies, nonprofit corporations, unions, homeowners and condominium associations) is that there's always a lawyer nearby. (That is a good thing, right?) Or look online for a reputable website that explains which laws affect specific meetings in your state.

Corporate Articles

If you're part of a nonprofit corporation, you shouldn't overlook the corporate articles (or *charter* or *articles of incorporation*). These days, the standard practice in most states is for the corporate articles to simply contain a few administrative details, such as the association's address and the name of the registered agent. However, procedural issues sometimes sneak into these documents. That can be a big deal because the corporate articles are one of the highest-governing documents for an incorporated nonprofit and typically supersede any bylaws. (See the following section for a discussion of bylaws.)

One association was planning its annual convention for October when it was noticed the articles of incorporation required a September meeting. Thankfully, there was time to change the meeting date (and the articles of incorporation were later amended).

Obviously, meeting in a month different than that required in the articles of incorporation would have violated the corporate documents. Even worse, it would have made the current officers (who were in contested elections) appear as though they were either not aware of the governing documents or ignoring the governing documents. Either would have looked bad and been made a campaign issue.

Other procedural issues that might appear in corporate articles include the method by which directors are elected and the required vote (majority or plurality).

Looking back at the hierarchy of authorities presented earlier in this chapter, you'll see that provisions in the corporate articles are generally lower and yield to statutes (unless the statute provides otherwise). However, the articles of incorporation can trump everything below them, such as the bylaws and other governing documents, in the event of a conflict.

Bylaws

In most organizations, bylaws are the highest-governing document that members have to concern themselves with regularly. There's a simple parliamentary rule for bylaws: *Follow them*. In fact, unless the bylaws have a specific provision, there is no "suspending" of the bylaws.

It used to be common practice for organizations to have two documents: a constitution and bylaws. The constitution contained the most important provisions and was very difficult to amend, while provisions in the bylaws were slightly easier to change. Because this often led to confusion and duplication, today's practice is to have one document named "bylaws" or the "constitution and bylaws." In older organizations or trade unions, you'll occasionally still see two documents or a single "constitution." In this book, the term "bylaws" refers to that document or documents, whatever the label.

Bylaws should include all the basic provisions of an organization. The bylaws define who the association is, what it can do, and how the organization is structured. While such a document includes far more than parliamentary practices, many procedural provisions are found in bylaws. In fact, one of the best ways to learn everything about a group quickly is to read the bylaws.

Officers, aspiring leaders, and anyone who wants to get things done in an organization should become familiar with the bylaws. While that might sound overwhelming (and possibly quite boring), good bylaws typically follow a standard order. Knowing what information falls where in bylaws can save you time when becoming familiar with an organization or trying to find a specific provision.

Here's the standard information you'll find in most bylaws in the order that they should appear in the document:

- **Name.** The first article should give the full name of the organization.

- **Object.** The object article should clearly state the objectives and boundaries of the association. According to *Robert's*, introducing a motion beyond the organization's object requires a two-thirds vote.

- **Members.** The members article contains information on membership types, qualifications for membership, financial obligations of members, rights of members, and procedures to remove members from the organization.

- **Officers.** The officers article tends to list the various offices and provides information on how officers are elected, the duties of specific offices, what to do in the event of a vacancy, and how to remove officers.

- **Meetings.** The meetings article contains everything from how often meetings are held, when they are held, where they are held, how the membership is notified of meetings, and what can be done at meetings. For larger associations, this section may contain details on conventions and delegates.

- **Executive Board.** If there is an executive board or board of directors, this article discusses how the board is selected, duties, when and how the board meets, and the board's authority. A clear description of the board's authority is essential. In some organizations, the board carries the full authority of the organization between member meetings and can act on all matters. In others, the board has limited powers and must bring decisions back to the members for review.

- **Committees.** Committees with a continuing existence throughout the year (known as "standing committees") should be listed in this article along with their responsibilities. (In contrast, "special committees" are created for specific tasks and terminate upon completion of their work.) Some bylaws simply provide that the membership or board may create committees as needed.

- **Parliamentary Authority.** This bylaws article prescribes a specific parliamentary book as the default meeting procedures. Most often, the language used is: "The rules contained in the current edition of [*Robert's Rules of Order Newly Revised*] shall govern the Association in all cases to which they are applicable and in which they are not inconsistent with these bylaws and any special rules of order the Association may adopt."

- **Amendment of Bylaws.** The last article usually provides the method of altering the bylaws. Most often, advance notice and a supermajority vote—such as two-thirds— are required.

Depending on the nature of the organization, there may be other articles. Some bylaws include provisions on finances, a smaller executive committee of the board of directors, state or local units of national associations, or disciplinary procedures. There is no one-size-fits-all set of bylaws that works for all organizations.

Special Rules of Order

As discussed earlier, not every rule in *Robert's* is perfect for every organization. Because of this, an organization can adopt *special rules of order* that supersede the general rule in the parliamentary authority. For instance, a convention might decide that the 10-minute speaking limit in *Robert's* is too long. If so, the convention can adopt a rule that speakers are limited to five minutes or two minutes (I've seen a 30-second rule adopted late in the afternoon on the last day of a long convention!)

Special rules of order are usually created in one of several ways. As mentioned earlier, conventions regularly adopt special rules of order (called "convention standing rules") to govern how convention delegates are recognized, how long they can speak in debate, how different motions are handled, and the process for nominating and electing officers. Such rules regulate certain parliamentary issues and are usually adopted by a two-thirds vote, but the vote can vary depending on the specific rule (see *Robert's*). In a typical member meeting or board meeting, a special rule of order can be adopted by a two-thirds vote with previous notice or a majority vote of the entire membership. Unlike bylaws, special rules of order can be suspended by a vote (either a majority or two-thirds, depending on the rule). Meeting rules should be placed in special rules of order and not bylaws to avoid confusion as to whether a rule can be suspended or not.

In Chapter 1, I mentioned that small boards can choose to be more formal procedurally, and that small assemblies might choose to operate less formally. Either option is accomplished through special rules of order.

Parliamentary Authority

By adopting a parliamentary authority, an organization commits to following the rules in that book. An article in the bylaws typically designates the parliamentary manual. If not, a parliamentary authority can be adopted through a special rule of order. Regardless of how designated, recognize that the parliamentary authority is at the bottom of the food chain, not the top. By running straight to *Robert's* or the designated parliamentary manual (and ignoring conflicting higher authorities, such as the bylaws or special rules of order), you may end up with the wrong answer.

Higher authorities than *Robert's* can include state law or governing documents. Provisions in such authorities that conflict with *Robert's* will likely prevail. The highest internal document for most organizations is the bylaws, which should be followed. Adopted special rules of order can also override *Robert's*.

Chapter 3

The Motion: How Things Are Done in Meetings

So far, we've discussed both formal and informal procedure at meetings. We really don't need to talk much more about being informal—just be informal! In contrast, formal procedure isn't quite as intuitive. So, let's talk about how business is accomplished in a formal setting. That includes large membership meetings, conventions, houses of delegates, or smaller boards that have decided to be more formal.

Everything Starts with a Motion

In a meeting following formal procedure, everything is done through *motions*, which are proposals by members to take action. And I do mean *everything*. You might have a motion to "renovate the association headquarters at a cost not to exceed $500,000." Or you might have a motion to "take a five-minute bathroom break." Either proposal is handled through a motion.

"Discussion first, motion later" might work for smaller bodies, but it usually leads to trouble in larger groups. For groups following formal procedure, nothing should occur without being preceded by a motion to take action.

Some groups like to talk about an issue for an hour, and then the chair asks, "Would someone like to make a motion?" The problem is, often nobody wants to make a motion. Sure, they were willing to talk about it for an hour, but they're not going to *do* anything about it. That might be fine for a committee or small board following informal procedure, but for a larger group, it's a wasted hour. Formal procedure is focused on accomplishing things, not just talking about things. A motion also gives you something specific to talk about. Because of this, business starts with a motion.

There are many different motions, and their characteristics vary. Some require a second, and some don't; some are debatable, and some aren't. For purposes of this book, the steps for considering a motion are fairly similar, regardless of the specific motion. Knowing the basic steps will make you a more effective member.

Bringing Forward a Motion

For most motions, a member must be recognized by the presiding officer before making the motion (later, we discuss motions that don't require recognition). Different groups allow members to be recognized in different ways. In conventions, delegates often have to go to a microphone and await recognition. In membership meetings, a member will likely just stand up at their place. In smaller groups following formal procedure, a raised hand might be all that is necessary. In virtual meetings, there tends to be an electronic feature for seeking recognition.

After a member who wants to make a motion is recognized, the motion goes through the following three steps.

(1) A Member Makes the Motion

Once the chair recognizes the member by stating the member's name or microphone number, the member makes the motion by stating, "I move that ...." For example, a motion might be, "I move that we Adjourn the meeting," or, "I move that we hire ABC Landscapers for the landscaping contract." Don't waste additional words. It's not, "I'd like to make a motion that we adjourn the meeting," or "I want to make a motion we hire ABC

Landscapers ….." All that's needed is, "I move that …," followed by what you wish the assembly to do.

Banish the phrase "I so move" from your vocabulary! "I so move" leads to confusion and uncertainty as to what was adopted. Generally, when a member says, "I so move," it means they liked what the prior speaker said, but they don't want to repeat it because it was complicated. That's why it should be repeated! Otherwise, the group is approving a concept but not the details needed to implement a motion. The maker should always state the motion as, "I move that …."

(2) Another Member Seconds the Motion

Once made, most motions require a second from another member to go forward. There are several misperceptions about seconds. First, a seconder doesn't have to support the motion. The seconder may hate it. The second is so the seconder can discuss what a lousy idea the motion is. A second merely means that another member feels the motion is worthy of discussion.

Seconds also aren't nearly as big of a deal as they're made out to be. A seconder can yell out "Second!" and doesn't even need to be recognized by the chair. The seconder's name doesn't go in the minutes. If, after some debate or a vote, it's realized the motion was never seconded, it doesn't matter. The assembly has already shown it wanted to discuss the matter. Motions from a committee don't need a second from the floor because they carry a second from the other members of the committee.

So, now that we've talked about how unimportant a second is, what exactly does it do? The requirement of a second is a gatekeeper. It simply lets the members know whether they should take the time to discuss an issue. When a motion is made, it is likely that another member will automatically yell out "SECOND!" If not, the chair should ask, "Is there a second?" If there is no second, the chair might want to ask a second time if there is a second. If there still is no response, the chair should state, "Because there is no second, that motion is not before us," and proceed to the next item of business.

Boards with fewer than 12 members typically don't require seconds. That makes sense if you consider the purpose of a second. In a group of 100, a second means that one person (the maker) and another (the seconder) want to discuss an issue. That's only 2 percent of the members. In a board of 4, any motion made already has the support of 25 percent of the members. Are you really going to require that 50 percent of the members want to talk about something before you discuss it?

(3) The Chair States the Question

The third and most important step occurs once a motion is made and seconded: The chair *states the question*. In *Robert's*, the term "question" is synonymous with the word "motion." "Stating the question" means "stating the motion." To state the question, the chair basically acts like a big parrot and repeats exactly what was moved as the motion. For example, "It is moved and seconded that the conference room be renovated at a cost not to exceed $50,000."

Why must the chair state the motion? First, this is the point where the chair can get the phrasing of the motion right. A motion is not what was said by a member but what is stated by the chair. The secretary is writing down the motion as repeated by the chair, and members in the audience can likely best hear the chair. This doesn't mean that the chair gets to make up the motion. Instead, the chair must listen carefully and state the motion correctly. Or the chair might need to help the maker phrase the motion better.

For example, a member might move "that the resolution be Laid on the Table until our next board meeting." Because the chair knows that a motion can't be tabled to a specific time, the chair might ask, "Is your intent to *Postpone* the motion until the next board meeting?" (which is a different motion altogether; see Chapter 5). If the member says "yes," then the chair states the question, "It is moved and seconded to Postpone the resolution until the next board meeting." (Why does the correct name of the motion matter? Because one motion, Postpone, is debatable, and the other, Lay on Table, is not. The chair just avoided a parliamentary mess!)

Also, when the chair states the question, a motion becomes official. Until a motion is stated by the presiding officer, the motion belongs to its maker. The maker could change the wording of the motion or say, "I've changed my mind. I'm taking my motion and going home." They can do this; it's their motion. However, once the chair says, "It is moved and seconded," the motion transfers from the maker to the body for discussion and a vote. At that point, the maker no longer "owns" the motion—the assembly does. If the maker wants to change the wording of the motion, they must ask the body for permission. If the maker wishes to withdraw the motion, they must obtain the assembly's consent.

Just as a member saying, "I so move" is bad, so is a chair saying, "You've heard the motion." That's a bad practice that should be corrected. The body hasn't officially heard the motion until the chair repeats it! A presiding officer should always clearly state any motion in full before allowing any discussion or vote.

Considering the Motion

Once the motion is stated by the chair and is on the floor, the deliberative process begins. That is, members can debate the motion to persuade other members to their position. Additional motions might even be proposed during debate (see Chapter 5). Finally, a vote will be taken on the motion, which is what it's all about. This is democracy in action!

Just as there are three steps for bringing forward a motion, there are three steps for considering a motion.

(1) Members Debate the Motion

Some motions are debatable; some aren't. (We talk about which motions are or are not debatable in Chapters 4 through 6.) If a motion is debatable, certain members get to speak before other members. They have "preference" in recognition. Not only do these recognition rules make sense, they might also save you time.

The maker of a motion speaks before anyone else. We want to hear why the motion is a good idea, so the chair calls on the maker first. Good presiding officers are on autopilot for this part of processing a motion. That is, once a motion is made and seconded, the chair states the question on the motion and immediately asks the maker, "Would you like to speak to your motion?"

Anyone who has not spoken gets to speak before anyone who has already spoken. We'd rather listen to six members one time than one member six times. In order to facilitate this, the chair might ask, "Is there someone who would like to speak who has not yet spoken?"

If possible, debate should alternate pro and con. This is one of the best timesavers in a meeting. After the maker of a motion speaks, the chair can ask, "Is there someone who would like to speak against the motion?" That way, we learn right up front if an issue is controversial. If no one wants to speak against the proposal, the chair might continue: "Seeing that no one wants to speak against the motion, is there any objection to closing debate and voting?" Without objection, the body can bypass discussion and move straight to a vote.

Other debate rules. Several other debate rules in *Robert's* might help your meeting. For instance, no one is permitted to speak a third time to a motion. You can speak a first time to a debatable motion. You don't get to speak again so long as anyone wants to speak a first time. After every member has had an opportunity to speak a first time, you can speak a second time to a motion.

Then you're done for the day as to that motion. Of course, you can speak twice to other motions. In other words, you could speak twice to a main motion, twice to a motion to Amend, and twice to a motion to Postpone. But on any specific motion, you can only speak twice per motion on the same day.

As mentioned, the maker of a motion has the right to speak first to the proposal. After that, however, the maker has no more right than anyone else with regard to the motion. In other words, the maker has no right to speak last in debate. Also, no one can speak against their own motion. A maker can ask permission to withdraw a motion or even vote against the motion. They just can't speak against it.

Another limit in *Robert's* is that no one can speak at one time for more than 10 minutes. Ten minutes is a *long* time. As a result, some groups and conventions adopt a special rule of order that limits debate even more, such as to five or three minutes per person at one time.

Rights in debate are not transferable. Unless an organization has a special rule, a member may not yield time to another member. Any such rule is almost always a bad idea, as it takes away the right to assign the floor from the chair and can lead to unfair results. (For instance, one member could be yielded to and speak four times in a row.) While the phrase "yield the floor" is sometimes used with reference to Congress or legislative bodies, such governmental entities follow their own rules and not *Robert's*.

(2) The Chair Puts the Question to a Vote

Eventually, debate will end (although sometimes, it might not feel that way), either because no one else wants to speak or because a motion to close debate has been adopted. At this point, the chair restates the motion to be voted on by saying, "The question is on the adoption of ..." and detailing the motion. That's right, the chair gets to be a big parrot again.

The purpose of "putting the question" is to make certain that everyone knows exactly what is being voted on. There's no worse situation than finding out after a vote that you thought you were voting on one motion but adopted (or defeated) a different one. Many meeting problems can be avoided by the chair carefully putting the question to a vote.

Various methods of voting and specific language for the chair are discussed in Chapter 7. For noncontroversial matters, unanimous consent can be the most efficient means of voting.

Unanimous consent (or "general consent") is a great timesaver for routine items. On motions that are likely noncontroversial, the chair can ask if there is any objection to approving the item. (For instance, "Is there any objection to closing debate?") If no one objects, the motion is approved. If a member objects, the presiding officer can take a formal vote.

Unanimous consent can even be used to take action without the formality of a motion. ("Is there any objection to taking a 10-minute recess?") If there is an objection, the chair can ask for a motion, seek a second, and process the motion formally.

(3) The Chair Announces the Vote

There are various methods of voting on a motion, including voice, rising, or show of hands. Whichever method is used, the final step in handling a motion is to announce the outcome of the vote. This step should not be overlooked or skipped, even if the outcome of the vote is apparent!

The full announcement on a vote varies depending on how the vote is taken. There is no magic language that MUST be used to announce the vote. However, *Robert's* has lots of examples of different vote announcements (that's one of the reasons the book is 714 pages long), so let me share some:

Voice vote (majority):

"The ayes have it, and the motion is adopted."

"The noes have it, and the motion is lost."

Rising vote (majority):

"The affirmative has it, and the motion is adopted."

"The negative has it and the motion is lost."

Rising vote (two-thirds)

"There are two-thirds in the affirmative, and the motion is adopted."

"There are less than two-thirds in the affirmative, and the motion is lost."

Ballot vote or count has been ordered:

"There are 101 in the affirmative and 90 in the negative. The affirmative has it, and the motion is adopted."

"There are 90 in the affirmative and 101 in the negative. The negative has it, and the motion is lost."

A final step in the announcement that good chairs include is to provide the consequence of the vote. In other words, if the motion being voted on is to "buy a copy of *Robert's* for every board member," the entire announcement of the voting result might be as follows:

"The ayes have it, and the motion is adopted. The Association will buy a copy of *Robert's* for every board member."

Repetition Is the Key to Success

The six steps for bringing forward a motion and then considering it might seem repetitive, but that's the point. One surefire way to lose control of a meeting is for members not to understand what is being discussed. Even worse is the situation in which members don't know what they're voting on. A primary purpose of proper procedure is to ensure that all members know the parliamentary situation.

In meetings following formal procedure, business is introduced through a motion. Steps vary for different motions. Most motions require that a member make the motion, another member second the motion, and for the chair to clearly state the question that is before the body. Motions are considered by being debated (if debatable), being put to a vote, and the chair announcing the result of the vote.

Chapter 4

The Main Motion

The main motion is where business almost always starts. That's because a main motion proposes a substantive item as a new subject. As such, main motions are the most common method of presenting matters to the body for discussion and action.

All of the following motions are examples of main motions:

> "I move that we purchase six copies of *Robert's Rules of Order.*"

> "I move that we renovate the corporate headquarters at a cost not to exceed $1 million."

> "On behalf of the committee, I move that next year's parliamentary procedure seminar be held in Hawaii."

In this chapter, I introduce you to the various types of main motions and the rules that govern them.

The Two Types of Main Motions

Very technically, there are two types of main motions:

- Original main motions
- Incidental main motions

Except in one instance, your parliamentary life likely won't be hindered if you don't know the difference. But *Robert's* differentiates, so let's take a look: An original main motion introduces a substantive item as new business when nothing else is pending. When the chair asks, "Is there any new business?" and a member responds with a motion, that is likely an original main motion.

In contrast, an incidental main motion proposes action of a parliamentary nature or related to substantive matters with which the assembly is already involved. Such motions tend to be "incidental" to business or the assembly's actions. For example, motions to Adopt the recommendations of a committee that was asked to consider an issue or a motion to Ratify actions taken at a previous meeting without a quorum are incidental main motions. Without getting too complicated here, an incidental main motion also includes procedural motions made when nothing else is pending. Chapter 5 will discuss secondary motions that are made when a main motion is pending. If they are made when no motion is pending, such motions are incidental main motions and are treated as main motions. Examples of such incidental main motions would include a motion to Refer a matter that is not pending, to Postpone a motion not before the body, or to Limit or Extend Limits of Debate for an entire meeting.

So, why do we care whether a main motion is an original main motion or an incidental main motion? Not to jump ahead of ourselves, but in Chapter 6, I talk about a motion named Objection to the Consideration of a Question, which allows an assembly to avoid discussion on a particularly undesirable main motion. Objection to the Consideration of a Question is only applicable to original main motions. The purpose behind Objection to Consideration makes no sense when it comes to incidental main motions. For incidental main motions arising out of committee or officer reports, the assembly has already been dealing with the motion, and it's too late to stop any involvement. For incidental main motions dealing with meeting procedure, Objection to the Consideration of a Question makes no sense, as that's not the type of discussion the motion is intended to prevent.

Two specific incidental main motions are the motion to Adopt and the motion to Ratify. Both deserve special mention. A motion to Adopt (or to Accept or to Agree to) a committee or officer's report is an incidental main motion if it involves matters referred to the committee or officer. Similarly, a motion to Ratify (or Approve or Confirm) is an incidental main motion used to validate an action previously taken under suspect circumstances. For example, a board might ratify an action taken at a previous meeting that was improperly called or lacked a quorum. Or an assembly could ratify a main motion adopted at a special meeting that was not included in the notice of the special meeting. Or an organization might ratify the actions of an officer, board, or committee that were in excess of the authority given to them in the governing documents.

Ratification should never be anticipated or relied upon in advance. For instance, as discussed in Chapter 9, if you have a meeting without a quorum, you should take steps to obtain a quorum or reschedule the meeting and not rely upon a subsequent meeting to ratify the improper actions of the previous meeting. That's because the organization might end up not ratifying the action. In such instances, the members who acted improperly can sometimes be held individually responsible for the action. Also, a body can only ratify an action that could have been approved in advance. In other words, an assembly can't ratify a motion after the fact that violated the bylaws or conflicted with a procedural rule in national, state, or local laws.

Like any main motion, the motion to Ratify is debatable and also opens the original issue to discussion.

Rules Regarding Main Motions

The rules regarding main motions are fairly straightforward:

- Main motions can only be moved when no other question is pending. In other words, no other motion can be on the floor when a main motion is introduced. If you've heard the saying, "There can't be two motions pending at the same time," that's not exactly true. You can have a main motion and many procedural secondary motions pending simultaneously, even though only one is the immediately pending question. What you can't have is two *main* motions pending at the same time.

- The maker of a main motion cannot interrupt business. That is, the maker must await recognition from the chair and cannot interrupt the process by attempting to make the motion while someone else is speaking.

- Main motions must be seconded in larger assemblies or bodies that follow more formal procedure (see Chapter 3).

- Main motions are debatable.

- Main motions are amendable.

- In most cases, main motions require a majority vote. The exceptions include when the bylaws might require more than a majority vote for certain types of action, such as amending governing documents, expulsion from membership, selling real property, or raising dues/assessments over a given amount. A main motion proposing to suspend a parliamentary rule or right, such as a motion to limit speeches during an entire meeting, will also likely require a two-thirds vote. Finally, if a main motion proposes to change something already adopted by the assembly, more than a majority vote might be required.

- Some main motions, such as bylaws, amendments, and a few procedural motions, require previous notice. Such notice must indicate the content of the motion and can be given orally at the preceding meeting for organizations that meet at least quarterly or can be included in the written notice of the meeting (referred to as the *call of the meeting*).

Avoiding Ambiguous Main Motions

Because adopted main motions are official actions of the assembly, they should be worded concisely and unambiguously. They should leave no room for interpretation. To avoid confusion, the following types of main motions should be avoided at all costs:

Motions to not do something. For instance, there is no need to adopt the motion "that we not send delegates to the international assembly." It's much simpler not to propose a motion to send delegates in the first place. In addition, if a motion to not do something is not adopted, it leaves you in the strange parliamentary situation of possibly having done something! For the same reason, it's best to avoid motions containing negative statements altogether. Instead of going on record as "not being in favor" of a political referendum, the assembly should "oppose" or "declare its opposition to" the referendum.

Motions to reaffirm a previous position. These types of motions can also lead to ambiguity. Generally, main motions adopted by an assembly remain in effect until changed or canceled by the assembly. They have a shelf life of forever. So, a motion to reaffirm a resolution from last year serves no useful purpose. In fact, it's more likely to lead to problems. If the assembly votes NOT to reaffirm the resolution, it makes for a very confusing parliamentary situation. The original resolution wasn't before the body and is still in effect, but by rejecting the motion to reaffirm, it's unclear whether the assembly chose to take a different position. Because of this, motions to reaffirm are out of order.

In addition, certain main motions are not in order. These include:

- **Main motions that conflict with the corporate charter, constitution, or bylaws.** However, a motion to Amend any of these documents would be in order.

- **Main motions that conflict with a procedural rule contained in federal, state, or local law.** So, if a state statute prescribes quorum for a particular body, no main motion would be in order to change the quorum.

- **Main motions that present substantially the same question as a motion that was considered and rejected earlier in the same session.** Such a motion can be renewed at a later session, or a motion to Reconsider (see Chapter 6) can be made later in the same meeting.

- **Main motions that conflict with a motion previously adopted and still in effect.** Once again, a motion to Reconsider can be made during the same meeting. At a later meeting, the motion to Rescind or to Amend Something Previously Adopted (see Chapter 6) can be made.

- **Main motions that conflict with or present substantially the same question as a motion temporarily, but not finally, disposed of, that remains within the control of the assembly.** This could include a motion that was referred to a committee or that has been tabled. (To bring such main motions back before the body, you can use procedural motions that are covered in Chapter 6.)

- **Main motions that propose action outside the scope of the organization's object as defined in the bylaws, unless permitted by a two-thirds vote.** Note that this two-thirds vote isn't to adopt the motion; it simply permits its discussion.

Resolutions

Some groups, particularly conventions of delegates, like to present original main motions in the form of resolutions. A resolution is simply a written main motion in a particular format in which the arguments for the motion are often included in the wording. *Robert's* spends some six pages going over the various details of resolutions, and I won't repeat them. But here's the short version: A resolution begins with the capitalized and italicized word *"Resolved,"* followed by a comma and the capitalized word "That" prior to the main motion. So, a short resolution might be: *"Resolved,* That the convention express its appreciation to the outstanding parliamentarian."

Most often, resolutions tend to be much lengthier. That's because most resolutions include a preamble consisting of several sentences or paragraphs that provide supporting statements for the resolution. *Robert's* advises against preambles to resolutions on the basis that any statements to gain support might also create opposition. For instance, a resolution endorsing one political candidate might be opposed by members who are offended by preamble clauses that criticize other candidates. Despite this warning, most resolutions out in the world tend to have a (sometimes lengthy) preamble. As a result, a resolution might read as follows.

Whereas, Mary Smith has served as Superintendent of the ABC School System since its creation;

Whereas, Mary Smith has directed the school system from turbulent years to academic excellence; and

Whereas, Mary Smith has announced her intent to retire at the end of the school year;

Resolved, That the ABC School System expresses its gratitude and appreciation to Mary Smith for her many years of outstanding service; and

> *Resolved*, That the ABC School System wishes Mary
> Smith a rewarding and restful retirement.

Robert's makes a distinction between general resolutions and resolutions that direct staff or employees to do something. In the latter, the word *"Ordered"* can be used in place of the word *"Resolved."* A resolution directed to an employee might end with: *"Ordered*, That the Executive Director obtain an immediate audit of the association's finances."

When considering a resolution, the language in the resolved clause is what really matters. In fact, many organizations don't include the preamble in the language of any adopted resolutions. It's important to determine whether the wording of the preamble matters before adoption. Some organizations have adopted resolutions only to be later embarrassed by a preamble provision that was presented to the media along with the resolution.

When a resolution has a preamble that is amendable, *Robert's* provides that the preamble should not be amended until after any resolved clauses have been amended. This is because changes to the resolved clauses might require changes to wording in the preamble. If a motion for the Previous Question (see Chapter 5) is adopted and closes debate on a resolution before the preamble has been considered for amendment, the motion to close debate does not apply to the preamble, which is then open to discussion and any amendments.

A main motion brings business before the assembly and can only be made when no other motion is pending. There are two kinds of main motions: *original main motions*, which introduce a substantive item as a new subject, and *incidental main motions*, which tend to be "incidental" to parliamentary procedure or the assembly's prior actions. There are many rules governing main motions, including when they can be introduced, their wording, and the vote required for adoption. Resolutions are main motions in a particular format, often with "Whereas" and "Resolved" clauses.

Chapter 5

The Most Frequently Used Motions

Chapter 4 focused on main motions, which are used to introduce substantive business. In theory, meetings could function with only main motions. A motion could be made "that ABC Pool Care be hired as the pool company." That main motion would be discussed and voted up or down. Another main motion could then be introduced, debated, and voted on. And then another.

But only being able to vote a proposal up or down isn't very efficient. After all, you might want to suggest a different pool company, refer the issue to a smaller group for study, or postpone the proposal. Such actions and more are possible through secondary motions. A secondary motion is a motion that can be considered while a main motion is pending. Secondary motions fall into three classes:

- **Subsidiary motions:** Assist in treating or disposing of the main motion.

- **Privileged motions:** Pertain to special matters of importance not relating to the main motion.

- **Incidental motions:** Pertain to procedural issues that arise incidentally and must be resolved before proceeding.

If you go hunting in *Robert's*, you can find more than 80 different types of secondary motions (but if you've actually done that, you might want to consider taking up a hobby). That's more motions than you'll ever need in a lifetime of meetings. Most meetings survive with about a dozen motions.

This chapter examines the most frequently used subsidiary and privileged motions, the specific rules for each, and how they work together. Chapter 6 explores incidental motions.

However, before delving into the details of various subsidiary and privileged motions, you need to understand how these secondary motions relate to one another and to other motions.

Following the Order of Precedence

Have you ever been at a meeting and heard the chair say, "That motion is out of order"? You might have thought, "Why is that motion out of order? It sounds just as good as anyone else's motion." Most likely, the motion was out of order because it was made at the wrong time. Some motions must precede other motions, which is known as the order of precedence. (The term is pronounced *pree-SEED-ens* and signifies that the consideration of some motions must precede other motions.) The order of precedence tells you two important things: when a motion is in order, and in what order to vote on pending motions.

First, the order of precedence tells you at any moment whether a particular motion is in order. I provide the order of precedence for the most common motions described in this chapter in the following Simplified Parliamentary Motions Guide (check out Appendix B for a more complete guide to motions).

Simplified Parliamentary Motions Guide

Motion	Second?	Debatable?	Amend?	Vote?
Adjourn	Yes	No	No	Majority
Recess	Yes	No	Yes	Majority
Table	Yes	No	No	Majority
Previous Question	Yes	No	No	Two-thirds

Motion	Second?	Debatable?	Amend?	Vote?
Limit Debate	Yes	No	Yes	Two-thirds
Postpone	Yes	Yes	Yes	Majority
Refer	Yes	Yes	Yes	Majority
Amend	Yes	Yes	Yes	Majority
Main Motion	Yes	Yes	Yes	Majority

A motion higher in rank (and higher up on the Simplified Parliamentary Motions Guide) than the immediately pending motion is in order and may be introduced, but a motion lower in rank is not in order and cannot be introduced. Here are some examples:

- While a main motion is pending, it is in order to move to Amend the main motion because the motion to Amend is higher in rank than the main motion.

- If a main motion and a motion to Amend are pending, a motion to Refer is in order because the motion to Refer is higher in rank than the motion to Amend.

- If a main motion and a motion to Recess are pending, a motion to Adjourn is in order because it is higher in rank than Recess. However, a motion to Refer wouldn't be in order because Refer is lower in rank than Recess.

When it's time to vote, the order of precedence also tells you what order to vote on the pending motions. Motions are voted on in reverse order from how they were made. In other words, let's suppose the following three motions are pending: Adjourn, Refer, and main motion.

The first vote is taken on the highest-ranking motion that is immediately pending—the motion to Adjourn. If the motion to Adjourn is adopted, the meeting is adjourned. If the motion to Adjourn is rejected, discussion is open on the motion to Refer. If the vote on the motion to Refer is eventually adopted, the entire issue is referred to committee. If the motion to Refer is rejected, the discussion is open again on the main motion. The final vote is on the main motion. However, before the vote on the main motion, other motions may be made, considered, and voted upon, so long as they are higher in rank than any pending motion. Another way to state the rule of precedence is that you can always go up the chart of motions, so long as you vote on the motions at the top before you come back down the chart.

The Subsidiary Motions

In this section, I explain each of the subsidiary motions along with its specific rules in a formal assembly. Keep in mind that some of the rules—such as the need for a second—might not apply in a smaller, informal board (see Chapter 3 for details).

Note: In the rules accompanying each motion, the terms *can interrupt* or *cannot interrupt* refer to whether the maker can interrupt other business to make the motion or whether they must be recognized by the chair to make the motion.

Postpone Indefinitely

Despite its name, the motion to Postpone Indefinitely doesn't postpone anything. It kills the main motion for the session. So why use this motion instead of simply voting against the main motion? The distinction is mainly one of appearances.

Let's suppose the main motion proposes to name the headquarters after a former executive director. The former executive director is a friend to most. However, many members don't believe it's appropriate to name the building after a living person. To vote against the main motion might be viewed as a rejection of the executive director. Postpone Indefinitely allows the assembly to avoid a direct vote on the main motion. If the motion to Postpone Indefinitely is adopted, the effect will be the same as defeating the proposal, but it sounds better than voting against the motion to name the headquarters after the executive director.

Here's a snapshot of the rules for Postpone Indefinitely:

❏ Cannot interrupt

❏ Needs a second

❏ Is debatable

❏ Isn't amendable

❏ Requires a majority vote

Debate on Postpone Indefinitely can go fully into the merits of the main question, which is unique. Debate on other subsidiary motions is limited to just the subsidiary motion. That is, with other secondary motions, you can't debate the main motion at the same time.

Amend

After main motions, the motion to Amend is the most frequently used motion. The purpose of an amendment is to somehow alter the wording of the main motion. There are several forms of amendment, including the following:

• To add or insert

• To strike (or strike out)

• To strike out and insert, such as replacing a name or number with another

• To substitute by replacing an entire paragraph, resolution, or main motion with other wording

Here are the rules governing the motion to Amend:

❑ Cannot interrupt

❑ Needs a second

❑ Is debatable

❑ Is amendable

❑ Requires a majority vote

In addition to these main rules, *Robert's* has many rules that are specific to each form of amendment. For instance, you can't use an amendment to change one type of motion to another. (That is, you can't amend a motion to Postpone Indefinitely by striking "Indefinitely" to simply postpone the motion.) Also, the motion to Amend requires a majority vote, regardless of the vote required to adopt the main motion. *Robert's* has more than 20 pages outlining specific rules for different types of amendments, which are beyond the scope of this book. However, if you're going to spend time with amendments in a formal parliamentary setting, you might want to review those pages.

Erroneous beliefs about amendments are common. You will sometimes hear that an amendment is out of order because it "changes the intent of the main motion." Yes, it does. That's what amendments do! If you were happy with the original intent, you wouldn't be making an amendment. Amendments can be hostile to or defeat the spirit of the original proposal. A motion to "support the campaign finance initiative" could be amended by moving to strike "support" and insert "condemn." To be in order, an amendment must simply be *germane* to the original proposal. To be germane means an amendment must involve the same question raised by the original motion. Determining whether an amendment is germane can be difficult and must sometimes be resolved by vote of the assembly.

At a meeting, you might hear a reference to a *friendly amendment*. Used properly, a friendly amendment is simply a method of adopting a noncontroversial amendment by unanimous consent. That is, a member may propose an amendment they believe will be accepted by the maker of the original proposal. If they're wrong and the maker rejects the amendment, the maker of the amendment can choose to propose the amendment formally. If the maker of the main motion accepts the amendment, the chair should ask the question of the assembly, "Is there any objection to the proposed amendment?" If not, the friendly amendment is adopted. If anyone objects, the maker of the amendment can decide whether or not to propose the amendment formally. This all goes back to the concept that after a motion is stated by the chair, it belongs to the assembly and not the original maker.

After an amendment is proposed, all discussion and attention should turn to the amendment. The main motion takes a backseat. When handling an amendment, the chair should focus like a laser on the specific words to be changed. Let's suppose the main motion is "that the clubhouse be renovated for a cost not to exceed $5,000." An amendment is made to strike "$5,000" and insert "$10,000." To state that the motion is "that the headquarters be renovated for a cost not to exceed $10,000" is incorrect and will lead to confusion. Discussion is no longer on whether to renovate the headquarters. The pending question is solely on the amendment to "strike $5,000 and insert $10,000."

When debate ends, a vote is taken on the amendment in the following form: "The question is on the adoption of the amendment to strike $5,000 and insert $10,000." If the amendment is rejected, the chair announces that the amendment is lost and that the group is back to discussion of the main motion as originally proposed. If the amendment is adopted, the chair states that fact and the question is now on the main motion "as amended."

You can have an amendment to a motion, known as the primary amendment, pending. You can also have an amendment to an amendment, known as the secondary amendment, pending. But that's it. Having more than a primary and secondary amendment would get too complicated. However, as amendments are resolved, other amendments can be proposed. Just keep in mind that you can never have more than two amendments—the primary and a secondary amendment—pending at a time.

With that in mind, it's worth considering what qualifies as an amendment to the amendment. Suppose the main motion is "to renovate Allen School at a cost not to exceed $100,000." While we are discussing the motion, someone moves to Amend by adding "and parking lot" after the word "School." That's germane. It looks like a fine primary amendment.

Following a second and being stated by the chair, discussion begins on just the amendment to add the words "and parking lot." During debate, a member notes that renovating the parking lot as well will cost more and moves "to Amend the amendment by changing $100,000 to $150,000."

Wait a minute. The amendment was to add the words "and parking lot" after the word "School." Changing the dollar amount doesn't have anything to do with those words. That's from a whole different part of the motion. A motion to change $100,000 to $150,000 isn't an amendment to the amendment. It's a different primary amendment and out of order while another primary amendment (to add the words "and parking lot") is pending.

If the amendment to add the words "and parking lot" is adopted, the body might want to consider an amendment to increase the amount of available money.

However, if the primary amendment to add the words "and parking lot" fails, there is likely no need to address the money issue. That's the beauty of primary and secondary amendments.

So what would be a proper secondary amendment? Let's revisit the primary amendment to add the words "and parking lot." Suppose the school has parking lots A, B, and C. While the primary amendment is pending, a secondary amendment might be made "to add 'C' after the word 'lot,'" so that the amendment would read "and parking lot C." Discussion on the secondary amendment is restricted to adding that one letter. If adopted, the primary amendment will be limited to renovating parking lot C. Regardless of how the vote on the secondary amendment goes, it's important to remember that the primary amendment and the main motion haven't been adopted. Only the secondary amendment has been resolved. You still have several motions and votes to go!

As mentioned earlier, *Robert's* has many specific rules governing amendments. While most other parliamentary authorities don't get nearly as complicated with secondary amendments, the rules exist in *Robert's*, so it's worth covering a few:

- An amendment to add or insert words can be amended by secondary amendment to add even more words or to strike words from the proposed primary amendment.

- An amendment to strike words can only be amended by secondary amendment to strike words from the primary amendment. The effect of such an amendment is to add the words back into the motion. (It's like a double negative—striking words to be stricken keeps them!)

- An amendment to strike a single word can't be amended.

- An amendment to strike out a paragraph has its own rules: the paragraph to be stricken is open to secondary amendments before the vote on the primary amendment to strike the entire paragraph. If the amendment to strike is adopted, the paragraph is gone. If the amendment to strike is defeated, the paragraph remains with any changes made by secondary amendment.

- The motion to substitute covers 10 pages in *Robert's*. Here's the two-sentence version: Both the substitute and the original main motion or resolution can be opened to amendment. Once both are made as good as possible, a vote is taken on whether to replace the original motion with the substitute language. This summary omits a few details, so check out *Robert's* if you plan to propose a substitute!

A process closely related to amendments is *filling blanks*. In filling blanks, a motion to select a name, place, date, or number or amount can be left blank. For example, "I move that dues be increased by ___ dollars." Or while a main motion is pending, a motion can be made to strike the name, place, date, or number (or amount) and to create a blank. Any number of alternatives can then be proposed and voted upon. The process of filling blanks allows more than two other options to be considered at one time. Because of the many details of filling blanks, you should refer to *Robert's* for specific rules.

Commit or Refer

The motion to Refer is used to send a main motion to a smaller group for consideration. If an amendment or amendments are pending, the motion to Refer applies to the main motion and any amendment(s). An amendment cannot be referred alone (without the main motion) unless a rule specifically permits such action.

Here are the rules at a glance for the motion to Refer:

❏ Cannot interrupt

❏ Needs a second

❏ Is debatable, but debate is limited to the issue of referral

❏ Is amendable as to the committee, its members, and any instructions to the committee

❏ Requires a majority vote

There are three highly technical uses of the motion to Refer that don't send the question to another group but instead, allow the assembly to consider the issue without normal debate rules applying. These variations are as follows:

- To go into a committee of the whole
- To go into quasi committee of the whole
- To consider informally

If your organization uses these techniques, you should read *Robert's*. (*Word of advice:* If your organization likes to go into committee or quasi committee of the whole, it might be time to join a new organization.)

Postpone to a Certain Time

The motion to Postpone to a Certain Time is used to delay consideration of a proposal. Such a delay can be until a certain date and time ("until our next board meeting") or until after a certain event ("until the Treasurer arrives"). For groups that meet at least as often as quarterly, a motion (and any pending motions) can be postponed as far as the end of the next meeting. However, you can't postpone something until "three meetings from now" because the motion will get lost.

As discussed in Chapter 11, a matter postponed until the following meeting becomes unfinished business on that meeting's agenda. Groups that only meet once a year, such as a convention, cannot postpone a matter to the next annual meeting.

The primary rules governing the motion to Postpone to a Certain Time are as follows:

- ❏ Cannot interrupt
- ❏ Needs a second
- ❏ Is debatable, but debate is limited to whether the main motion should be postponed
- ❏ Is amendable as to when the matter should be postponed
- ❏ Requires a majority vote

Limit or Extend Limits of Debate

The motion to Limit or Extend Limits of Debate allows the assembly to place parameters on the discussion of the pending motion. Without such a motion, debate is limited to 10 minutes per person at one time, and no one can speak more than twice to a single motion (see Chapter 3 for details and exceptions). The motion to Limit or Extend Limits of Debate can be used to shorten debate for each speaker, such as "three minutes per speaker." The motion can also be used to limit total debate, such as "no more than one hour on the main motion and any secondary motion" or even "three speakers pro and three speakers con."

Here are the rules governing the motion to Limit or Extend Limits of Debate:

- ❏ Cannot interrupt
- ❏ Needs a second
- ❏ Is not debatable
- ❏ Is amendable
- ❏ Requires a two-thirds vote

The motion to Limit or Extend Limits of Debate is not debatable but is amendable. That is, there might be alternate proposals for structuring debate. Any amendments, like the motion, are undebatable. Because speaking rights are being affected, the motion to Limit or Extend Limits of Debate requires a two-thirds vote.

Previous Question (Close Debate)

The motion for the Previous Question is the ultimate limiting of debate. That is, the motion is a fancy way of saying, "I want to close debate and vote now." Some parliamentary authorities call this motion by the more descriptive "Close Debate and Vote

Immediately." The motion can also be applied to motions that are amendable but not debatable (to stop amendments).

The rules for the motion for the Previous Question are as follows:

- ❏ Cannot interrupt
- ❏ Needs a second
- ❏ Is not debatable
- ❏ Is not amendable
- ❏ Requires a two-thirds vote

The motion isn't debatable because it would be confusing to debate whether or not we don't want to debate.

Robert's expressly provides that a member may speak to a motion and conclude his remarks by moving the Previous Question. However, this tactic almost always annoys other members. Some organizations adopt a special rule of order that a member speaking to a motion cannot conclude by moving the Previous Question.

The motion for the Previous Question applies only to the immediately pending question. So, if an amendment is being discussed, a member moving the Previous Question is asking that debate cease and a vote be taken on the amendment. However, the motion for the Previous Question can also be made in qualified form, which means to move the Previous Question on the immediately pending motion and any consecutive motion. The Previous Question can even be moved on all pending motions.

The motion for the Previous Question is the most mishandled of all motions. First, the motion cannot interrupt a speaker. No one can yell out "Question!" from the back of the audience and expect anything to happen (except perhaps the question from the chair, "Do you have a question?"). A member who wants to close debate must be recognized by the chair and make the motion by saying, "I move the Previous Question" or "I call the Question." The exact words aren't as important as the chair determining that the intent of the member is to close debate.

The second situation in which Previous Question gets mishandled is in the vote. At times, a member will move or call the Previous Question, and the chair responds with, "The Previous Question has been called. Debate is closed." Wait a minute! A vote must always be taken to close debate. (Of course, that vote might be by unanimous consent. On noncontroversial matters, the chair can always ask, "Is there any objection to closing debate and voting on the motion to _____? Hearing no objection, debate is closed.")

Table

Lay on the Table allows an assembly to temporarily set a motion (and any pending motions) aside when another urgent matter has arisen. The strange name of the motion comes from the legislative practice of laying a bill on the clerk's table to await further consideration. Some other parliamentary authorities refer to this motion by the more descriptive *Postpone Temporarily*. Here are the rules:

- ❏ Cannot interrupt
- ❏ Needs a second
- ❏ Is not debatable
- ❏ Is not amendable
- ❏ Requires a majority vote

After the motion for the Previous Question, the motion to Lay on the Table is the most misused motion. My simple rule for determining when the motion to Table is being used incorrectly at a meeting is this: whenever the motion to Table is used at a meeting, it is used incorrectly. Okay, that rule might overstate things a bit, but not by much.

Most groups that use the motion to Table have no intention of ever revisiting the main motion. They want it gone for good. *Robert's* is clear that using the motion to Table like this is improper and should be ruled out of order. Why? Because the motion to Table isn't debatable and only requires a majority vote. It's unfair to kill something with only a majority vote and no debate. Rather than use the motion to Table, members should speak against the main motion and vote against it.

So, what's a proper use of the motion to Lay on the Table? Suppose during debate, the governor arrives. The motion to Lay on the Table would allow the body to quickly set aside the pending business to allow the governor to address the organization. After the governor leaves, the body can take the issue from the table (see Chapter 6).

Another use of Lay on the Table might be to address a medical or meeting emergency. The point here is that the motion to Lay on the Table should only be used to temporarily set aside a main motion so that something urgent can be addressed, after which the main motion will come back on the floor.

If a matter is laid on the table and not removed, it remains there until the end of the next meeting (so long as it is within a quarterly interval). If not removed by that time, the question dies. Conventions or organizations that do not meet at least quarterly cannot lay a matter on the table to the following meeting.

The Most Used Privileged Motions

Privileged motions are not related to the pending business, but involve issues important enough to take priority over the main motion and any pending subsidiary motions. Such an issue might be the distraction to members caused by an uncomfortably chilly room. Or maybe the members want to take a short bathroom break or even end the meeting.

Here are the four most common privileged motions.

Raise a Question of Privilege

To Raise a Question of Privilege means to raise a request or motion relating to the rights and privileges of the assembly or the members. Most often, such requests don't require a motion or vote. Instead, the chair simply addresses the problem.

There are two types of questions of privilege: questions of privilege affecting the assembly and questions of personal privilege. The distinction usually doesn't matter. However, questions of privilege of the assembly take precedence over those of personal privilege. Questions of privilege of the assembly are the most common and might be raised when something is preventing members from full participation in the meeting (such as it's too hot, cold, or noisy). In contrast, questions of personal privilege relate to the individual and might relate to concerns about a statement made about the member earlier in the meeting. Too often, you'll hear members use "points of personal privilege" to make announcements, but that's an improper use of the motion.

The rules governing the motion to Raise a Question of Privilege are as follows:

- ❏ Can interrupt
- ❏ No second required
- ❏ Isn't debatable
- ❏ Isn't amendable
- ❏ No vote

Occasionally, a chair won't rule on a question of privilege but will allow it to be introduced as a motion (for instance, to allow a guest to speak to an issue). In such instances, the main motion admitted as a question of privilege requires a second, is debatable, amendable, and takes a majority vote.

Recess

The motion to Recess permits a short intermission, usually not longer than a bathroom break or a meal. Business is picked back up following a recess right where it was left off.

Ready for the rules for the motion to Recess? Here they are:

- ❏ Cannot interrupt
- ❏ Needs a second
- ❏ Isn't debatable
- ❏ Is amendable
- ❏ Requires a majority vote

While a motion to Recess isn't debatable, it is amendable. Another member might have a different idea of how long the break should be. Any such amendment is undebatable. If a motion to Recess is made when nothing is pending, it isn't a subsidiary motion; instead, it's a main motion that is debatable.

Adjourn

The motion to Adjourn ends a meeting. In a multiday convention, the motion to Adjourn may also be used to end each day's session. Unlike a recess, the assembly typically reconvenes from an adjournment with some introductory ceremonies. In organizations that meet regularly, the motion to Adjourn is always treated as a privileged motion and is governed by the following rules:

- ❏ Cannot interrupt
- ❏ Needs a second
- ❏ Isn't debatable
- ❏ Isn't amendable
- ❏ Requires a majority vote

Several parliamentary steps are in order while a motion to Adjourn is pending, including notifying the assembly of business requiring attention or important announcements, making a motion to Reconsider, giving notice of a motion requiring previous notice, and moving to Fix the Time to Which to Adjourn (discussed next).

Only in the following situations is the motion to Adjourn treated as a main motion:

- If the motion to Adjourn is qualified, as in adjourning at or to a future time
- If a time for adjournment is already established through a program or adopted motion
- When the motion to Adjourn will dissolve the assembly with no provision for another meeting, such as the last day of a convention

In such instances, the motion to Adjourn is debatable, amendable, and out of order if anything else is pending.

Fix the Time to Which to Adjourn

The motion to Fix the Time to Which to Adjourn is the means for establishing an adjourned meeting (see Chapter 9). The motion has nothing to do with when the present meeting adjourns. In fact, if adopted, the meeting continues uninterrupted. However, upon adjournment, the meeting will reconvene at a specific date and time for a continuation of the current meeting. The phrasing of this motion is usually to the effect: "I move that when we adjourn, we adjourn to meet next Saturday at 9 A.M."

Many meeting-goers will live out their parliamentary lives without ever encountering this highest-ranked privileged motion. Even so, Fix the Time to Which to Adjourn has its uses. A sudden power outage might require a meeting to be continued to another date. A situation in which quorum is lost during discussion of a motion is another example. The members might want to resume the meeting another day in hopes of better attendance.

Note: Fix the Time to Which to Adjourn can be made even when there is no quorum. Also, the high precedence of this motion enables it to be made after the assembly has voted to adjourn, so long as the chair has not declared adjournment.

Here are the rules governing the motion to Fix the Time to Which to Adjourn when it is privileged:

❑ Cannot interrupt

❑ Needs a second

❑ Isn't debatable

❑ Is amendable as to the time and place of the meeting

❑ Requires a majority vote

The motion to Fix the Time to Which to Adjourn is only privileged if made while a main motion is pending. Otherwise, it is a main motion. The privileged motion to Fix the Time to Which to Adjourn is not debatable but is amendable as to the time and place of the meeting. Such amendments are not debatable.

The Subsidiary and Privileged Motions in Action

Now that we've examined the most used subsidiary and privileged motions, let's look at how they work together at a meeting. You might want to follow along with the Simplified Parliamentary Motions Guide from earlier in this chapter.

Warning: The following example contains many more motions than you would see at any typical meeting. If you can work through the example without your eyes rolling into the back of your head, you have mastered the concept of precedence.

Suppose the main motion being discussed is to renovate the clubhouse at a cost not to exceed $50,000.

A motion is made to Amend the motion by striking "$50,000" and inserting "$25,000" (which is in order as the motion to Amend is higher on the list). Discussion begins on the amendment.

A motion is made to Refer the matter to the Building and Grounds Committee (which is in order). Discussion begins on the motion to Refer.

A motion is made to Postpone the matter until next month's board meeting (which is in order).

A member then moves to Adjourn (which is in order).

Prior to voting on the motion to Adjourn, a member obtains the floor and moves to Recess for 5 minutes.

The motion to Recess is out of order in that it is lower in the order of precedence than the motion to Adjourn.

The pending motions are considered in reverse order (from highest to lowest). In other words, a vote is taken on the motion to Adjourn.

If the motion passes, the meeting ends, and everyone goes home.

If the motion to Adjourn fails, the assembly considers the motion to Postpone.

If the motion to Postpone passes, consideration of the matter ends in that it has been postponed.

If the motion to Postpone fails, the assembly considers the motion to Refer.

If the motion to Refer passes, consideration of the matter ends in that it has been sent to committee.

If the motion to Refer fails, the assembly considers the motion to Amend.

The proposed amendment (to change the amount) will pass or fail.

Finally, the assembly considers and votes on the main motion to renovate the clubhouse (either as originally proposed or as amended, depending on the outcome of the amendment).

Before the final vote on the main motion, other motions may be introduced and considered, so long as they are higher in order of precedence than the pending motion.

Motions tend to fall into one of three classes:

- *Subsidiary motions* help perfect or dispose of the main motion.
- *Privileged motions* pertain to special matters of importance not related to the main motion.
- *Incidental motions* involve procedural issues.

The order of precedence tells you when a motion is in order as well as in what order to vote on all pending motions. While there are many motions in *Robert's*, Subsidiary motions are the most frequently used and are to Postpone Indefinitely; Amend; Commit (or Refer); Postpone to a Certain Time; Limit or Extend the Limits of Debate; Previous Question (Close Debate); and Table. The most used Privileged motions are to Raise a Question of Privilege, Recess, Adjourn, and Fix the Time to Which to Adjourn. Each motion has rules as to whether it can interrupt, requires a second, whether the motion is debatable or amendable, and what vote is required.

Chapter 6

Other Motions You Need to Know

Unlike the subsidiary and privileged motions (see Chapter 5), the motions in this chapter have no order of precedence. Incidental motions arise during business as needed and are resolved immediately. Similarly, the four motions classified as Motions that Bring a Question Again Before the Assembly do exactly what their name suggests—they allow the body to revisit an issue considered at an earlier time. Included in this chapter are some of the most powerful motions for protecting members' rights. It's worth finding out about their use and specific rules.

Incidental Motions

Incidental motions tend to be incidental to the business at hand. That is, they generally don't directly involve the main motion but are related more to process and procedure (such as a motion to demand a rising vote following a voice vote). Because these motions are time-sensitive, they can often interrupt business, might not require a second, and might not even require a vote.

In the following sections, I introduce you to the most frequently used incidental motions and provide you with an at-a-glance look at their procedural rules.

Point of Order

A Point of Order points out a possible procedural error at a meeting and requests a ruling and enforcement of the rules from the chair. A Point of Order can arise from a violation of governing documents or a parliamentary procedure error. (Note: Points of Order are intended to address procedural problems and not factual misstatements during debate. If a member feels that something said in debate was in error, the proper course is not to raise a Point of Order, but to provide correct information through debate.)

The rules for a Point of Order are as follows:

❏ Can interrupt

❏ No second required

❏ Isn't debatable

❏ Isn't amendable

❏ No vote required

The motion can interrupt other business because we don't want to wait an hour to find out that we did something wrong. Unlike most of the motions discussed so far, a Point of Order needs no second, is not debatable, and requires no vote. Instead, the chair simply rules on the Point of Order.

If in the middle of debate, the chair hears a quiet "Point of Order" from the back of the room, everything stops until the issue is resolved. The chair should ask, "What is the Point of Order?" The member might explain that a new main motion is being discussed without ever having voted on the last one. No discussion or vote is needed because one of two things is going to happen: The chair might say, "The Point of Order is well taken," and explain that the vote on the last motion was mishandled and will be corrected immediately. Or the chair might say, "The Point of Order is not well taken," and explain that the previous motion was voted on by voice, then by a standing vote, and then by a count, all of which failed.

If a member doesn't like the chair's ruling on a Point of Order, the next motion is likely to be an Appeal (see the next section).

Because there are always going to be minor procedural errors in a meeting, it is important to distinguish between mistakes that matter and ones that don't. Not every tiny technical fault should lead to a Point of Order. As noted by General Henry M. Robert (the original author of *Robert's Rules*), "It is a mistake to be constantly raising points of order in regard to little irregularities …. The assembly meets to transact business, not to have members exploit their knowledge of parliamentary law. A business meeting is not a class in parliamentary law."

An important and useful aspect of Point of Order is the finality it brings to procedural disputes. *Robert's* has strict timeliness requirements for Points of Order. "If a question of order is to be raised, it must be raised promptly at the time the breach occurs." In other words, you can't sit through two motions and then complain there was no second to an earlier motion. Similarly, you can't argue at next month's meeting that a motion for the Previous Question was mishandled at this meeting. It's just too late. Most Points of Order that aren't raised promptly are waived.

There are a few exceptions to the requirement that a Point of Order must be raised immediately. First, because votes aren't supposed to be interrupted, a Point of Order regarding an error in or during voting can be raised immediately following the announcement of the vote. Second, some violations are of a continuing nature, in which case, a Point of Order can be made at any time during the continuance of the breach. Here are some examples of such instances:

- A main motion has been adopted that conflicts with the bylaws.

- A main motion has been adopted that conflicts with a previously adopted main motion still in force unless the second motion was adopted by the vote necessary to Rescind or Amend Something Previously Adopted (see later in this chapter).

- The assembly's actions violated a procedural rule in federal, state, or local law.

- The assembly's actions violated a fundamental principle of parliamentary law (see *Robert's* for examples).

- The assembly's actions violated a rule protecting absentees, a bylaws provision requiring a vote to be taken by ballot, or a rule protecting basic rights of an individual member (such as preventing a member from attending meetings unless there has been a disciplinary proceeding).

There might be occasions (hopefully rare) when the chair simply can't determine how to rule on a Point of Order. In such instances, the chair can refer the Point of Order to the judgment of the assembly. That is, the question is given to the body to debate and decide by a majority vote.

Appeal

As noted in the previous section, a member who is dissatisfied with a ruling of the chair can Appeal. To do so, the member states, "I Appeal from the decision of the chair." Once seconded, an Appeal is the most powerful motion in parliamentary procedure. After all, it takes the procedural ruling away from the chair and gives it to the members. At the end of the day, the body is the ultimate decider of all parliamentary decisions. The motion to Appeal brings home the idea that the chair is the servant of the assembly, not its master.

The rules for an Appeal are as follows:

❏ Can interrupt

❏ Needs a second

❏ Debate varies

❏ Isn't amendable

❏ Requires a majority vote

Appeals must be from a decision or ruling of the chair. As a result, no appeal can be made from the chair's answer to a Parliamentary Inquiry because that is simply an opinion (no ruling was made). Similarly, there can be no appeal from the chair's announcement of the result of a voice or standing vote. There are other procedural motions for challenging votes.

Debate on an Appeal varies, depending on the parliamentary situation. Most often, an Appeal is debatable. However, that is not the case if the Appeal relates to indecorum or a transgression of speaking rules, the priority of business, or if the Appeal is made when the pending question is undebatable. Even when debatable, the rules of debate on an Appeal vary from other motions. No member may speak more than once, except for the presiding officer, who may speak first and last. The presiding officer may also remain in the chair to debate because an official ruling has been challenged.

The wording of an Appeal is also a bit unusual. The question should not be "in favor of the Appeal," which would be confusing. Instead, the chair states the question as follows: "The question is, 'Shall the decision of the chair stand as the judgment of the assembly?' Those in favor of sustaining the chair's decision, say 'aye.' Those opposed to sustaining the decision, say 'no.' The decision is [is not] sustained." A majority vote in the negative is required to overrule the decision of the chair.

The motion to Appeal seems focused on the actions of the presiding officer. However, because any two members (a maker and a second) can appeal a decision of the chair, *Robert's* states an interesting rule: "Members have no right to criticize a ruling of the chair unless they appeal from his decision."

Suspend the Rules

The motion to Suspend the Rules allows the assembly to do something that would otherwise violate a procedural rule. For instance, a motion to Suspend the Rules could be adopted to allow a nonmember to discuss a motion. It's important to note that the motion to Suspend the Rules refers to rules in *Robert's*, known as special rules of order or convention rules. Bylaws generally cannot be suspended.

Here are the rules for the motion to Suspend the Rules:

- ❏ Cannot interrupt
- ❏ Needs a second
- ❏ Isn't debatable
- ❏ Isn't amendable
- ❏ Requires a two-thirds vote

The motion to Suspend the Rules most often requires a two-thirds vote. There are a few exceptions, which can become complicated. Rules protecting absentees (such as a rulesetting quorum) cannot be suspended, even by a unanimous vote. That's because the members protected by the rule aren't at the meeting. Similarly, rules protecting a basic right of individual members, such as the right of a member to attend meetings, cannot be suspended except through disciplinary proceedings or bylaws language. Finally, some convention rules can be suspended by only a majority vote. However, to suspend both the convention rule and any rules in *Robert's*, you're likely back to a two-thirds vote. Because of their complexity, motions like Suspend the Rules give parliamentarians job security.

The Standard Code of Parliamentary Procedure recognizes an interesting use of the motion to Suspend the Rules called the Gordian Knot motion. If the parliamentary situation has become so confused that no one is sure how to proceed, the motion to Suspend the Rules can be used to cancel out what's been done and restart the motion with a clean slate.

Objection to the Consideration of a Question

In Chapter 4, we discussed the differences between original and incidental main motions. (Granted, you might have suppressed those memories.) Objection to the Consideration of a Question permits an assembly to avoid considering an original main motion altogether. While not regularly seen at meetings, Objection to Consideration is so often mishandled that it deserves mention.

Ready for the rules for the motion to Objection to Consideration of a motion? Here they are:

❏ Can interrupt

❏ No second needed

❏ Isn't debatable

❏ Isn't amendable

❏ Requires a two-thirds vote against motion

Objection to Consideration must be made before any debate on the main motion. For this reason, a member who wants to object can interrupt and make the motion, even without recognition from the chair. Like an Appeal, the wording of the vote on the motion might seem somewhat backward. The vote is always whether to consider the main motion (not on sustaining the objection).

In other words, the chair should say: "The consideration of [New Business Item #5] is objected to. Shall [New Business Item #5] be considered? Those in favor of considering it, rise .... Be seated. Those opposed to considering [New Business Item #5], rise ...." To sustain the objection, a two-thirds vote against consideration is required.

As a result, the chair might say: "There are two-thirds opposed, and [New Business Item #5] will not be considered," or "There are less than two-thirds opposed, and the objection is not sustained. The question is on [New Business Item #5] ...."

Division of a Question

The name likely gives it away, but Division of a Question permits the assembly to divide a divisible motion. Emphasis is on the word *divisible*. A motion cannot be divided if its separate parts cannot stand alone. That is, a motion "to obtain a rental car for the officers and pay for all gasoline" is indivisible. Without the car, there is no need for gasoline. On the other hand, a motion "that we give the outgoing president a gavel, and that we give the outgoing secretary a pen" is divisible. *Robert's* provides that the division "cannot require a rewriting of the resolution beyond an essentially mechanical separation of it into the required parts."

The rules for the Division of a Question motion are as follows:

- ❏ Cannot interrupt
- ❏ Needs a second
- ❏ Isn't debatable
- ❏ Is amendable
- ❏ Requires a majority vote

The act of dividing a motion usually requires a majority vote (or unanimous consent). However, some motions must be divided upon the request of a single member. For instance, if a series of independent resolutions dealing with different subjects is offered in one large motion, one or more of the several resolutions must be separated at the request of a member.

Division of the Assembly

While Division of a Question and *Division of the Assembly* might sound similar, Division of the Assembly is simply a method of verifying a vote. The name of the motion comes from an older practice where those in favor and those opposed to a motion were "divided" by standing at opposite sides of the room. Today, a Division is taken simply by members standing at their places.

Whenever a member questions the result of a voice or show of hands vote, they can call out "Division." Such a demand requires that the chair retake the vote by an uncounted rising vote (see Chapter 7).

Here are the rules for a Division of the Assembly:

- ❏ Can interrupt
- ❏ No second needed
- ❏ Isn't debatable
- ❏ Isn't amendable
- ❏ No vote required

Parliamentary Inquiry

A Parliamentary Inquiry is a question to the chair on a matter of parliamentary procedure or the rules of the organization. Such requests aren't made nearly enough and could help resolve procedural issues before they become a problem.

- "What vote is required on this motion?"
- "If I want to delay this matter to our next board meeting, what motion should I use?"
- "What do our bylaws say with regard to suspending a member?"

The rules are as follows:

- ❏ Can interrupt if urgent
- ❏ No second needed
- ❏ Isn't debatable
- ❏ Isn't amendable
- ❏ No vote required

Request for Information

If *Request for Information doesn't sound familiar,* that might be because it's a new name for an old practice. Prior to the 11th Edition of *Robert's,* the method of requesting information on the pending motion was known as a Point of Information. The problem with that title was that some members would use it to give points of information (that is, debate), rather than ask for information. So, the preferred name of the motion changed from "Point of Information" to "Request for Information." Habits are difficult to change, so you'll still hear both phrases. A Request for Information should sound like a reporter's question and start with one of the five Ws: who, what, where, when, and why? "How" is okay, too. For example: "When will the dues increase take effect?" "What is the cost estimate for Resolution 6?"

Preferably, the question is not one the questioner already knows the answer to. Rhetorical questions are best left to debate.

Here are the rules for a Request for Information:

❏ Can interrupt if urgent

❏ No second needed

❏ Isn't debatable

❏ Isn't amendable

❏ No vote required

Motions That Bring a Question Again Before the Assembly

The four motions discussed in this section just don't fit well anywhere else. They all relate to revisiting an issue the assembly decided at an earlier time. As a result, they've been given the suitable (if somewhat long) title of Motions That Bring a Question Again Before the Assembly. Without question, these are some of the most confusing motions you'll encounter in your parliamentary adventure. For instance, the motion to Reconsider takes up 22 pages in *Robert's!*

So you won't give up parliamentary procedure forever, I'm just going to point out some basics of these motions. If you have to deal with any specific motion, you better check out *Robert's*.

Take from the Table

The motion to Lay on the Table temporarily sets aside a main motion (see Chapter 5), and the motion to Take from the Table brings it back. As discussed in Chapter 5, such action is often taken by unanimous consent ("Is there any objection to Taking from the Table ...?"), but the formal motion can also be used. The motion to Take from the Table can only be made when no other motion is pending. A motion can be taken from the table at the same meeting or the next, so long as the meeting is within the quarter. If it's not taken from the table by the close of that meeting, the question dies (and would have to be reintroduced). Any main motion taken from the table is resumed exactly at the point where it was laid on the table.

As to how soon the motion can be made, a motion to Take from the Table is not in order immediately after a question has been laid on the table. Some business or interrupting matter must have transpired since the motion to Lay on the Table was adopted.

The rules guiding the motion to Take from the Table are as follows:

- ❏ Cannot interrupt
- ❏ Requires a second
- ❏ Isn't debatable
- ❏ Isn't amendable
- ❏ Requires a majority vote

Rescind/Amend Something Previously Adopted

The motion to Rescind/Amend Something Previously Adopted is really two motions in one. The motion to Rescind (also known as Repeal or Annul) is used to cancel a previously adopted main motion.

The motion to Amend Something Previously Adopted is used to modify a previously adopted main motion. Unlike the motion to Reconsider (discussed later in this chapter), the motion to Rescind/Amend Something Previously Adopted can be moved by anyone, regardless of how they voted on the original motion.

The motion to Rescind/Amend Something Previously Adopted has no time limit. As mentioned in Chapter 12, meeting minutes could be corrected years after the fact through a motion to Amend Something Previously Adopted. The motion is debatable, and debate can go into the merits of the question proposed to be rescinded or amended.

Here are the rules for the motion to Rescind/Amend Something Previously Adopted:

- ❏ Cannot interrupt
- ❏ Requires a second
- ❏ Is debatable
- ❏ Is amendable
- ❏ Type of vote required varies

A few actions cannot be rescinded or amended. For instance, if something has been done that is impossible to undo, it is too late to make this motion. (For example, the event has already been held or property has already been purchased.) While rather technical, the motion to Rescind/Amend Something Previously Adopted also cannot be made if there has been a prior motion to Reconsider (discussed later in this chapter) on the same subject, and it is not too late to consider the motion to Reconsider.

Finally, this is not the correct motion when a resignation has been acted on or a person has been elected to or expelled from membership or office and already notified of the action. All such actions would require that the steps in the bylaws be followed.

The vote required on a motion to Rescind/Amend Something Previously Adopted can depend on the specific issue. For instance, if the motion proposes to change bylaws or other governing documents, the required vote will be that required by the documents (most often a two-thirds vote). In other instances, the motion to Rescind/Amend Something Previously Adopted requires any of the following votes:

- ❏ A two-thirds vote
- ❏ A majority vote if previous notice of the motion has been given
- ❏ A majority vote of the entire membership

Governmental boards often transact business through the motion to Amend Something Previously Adopted, although that name will likely not be used. Any motion to Amend an existing policy or modify rules would qualify. Since governmental bodies typically require advance notice of motions, only a majority vote is required. Even if prior notice wasn't required, most board members attend such meetings, and a majority vote of the entire board would be sufficient as another method.

Discharge a Committee

The motion to Refer (see Chapter 5) sends a main motion to a smaller group for consideration, and the motion to Discharge a Committee brings it back. Except for this motion, an assembly is prevented from considering a motion involving practically the same question as one being considered by a committee. Despite its name, the motion to Discharge a Committee doesn't typically do away with a committee; instead, it simply takes back a referred item.

Here are the rules:

- ❏ Cannot interrupt
- ❏ Requires a second
- ❏ Is debatable
- ❏ Is amendable
- ❏ Type of vote required varies

The motion can only be made when nothing else is pending; it is debatable, and debate can go into the merits of the question in the hands of the committee.

The vote on a motion to Discharge a Committee varies depending on the circumstances. Because this motion changes action previously taken by the assembly, the motion to Discharge a Committee requires any of the following votes:

- ❏ A two-thirds vote
- ❏ A majority vote if previous notice of the motion has been given
- ❏ A majority vote of the entire membership

Only a majority vote is required if the committee fails to report when instructed or if the committee is giving a partial report at the time.

Encountering the motion to Discharge a Committee is rare. However, it's a valuable motion if a committee has failed to act on something referred to it.

Reconsider

Instead of saving the best for last, we have the motion to Reconsider. You won't find a more confusing or convoluted motion. However, it has its uses. Specifically, the motion to Reconsider is designed to allow an assembly to revisit a motion (whether adopted or rejected) within certain time frames. While the motion that is the subject of a motion to Reconsider is often a main motion, various subsidiary and incidental motions may be reconsidered. (Although some other parliamentary authorities limit the motion to Reconsider to main motions only.)

Some motions can only be reconsidered depending on the outcome of the earlier vote. For instance, only an affirmative vote on the motion to Postpone Indefinitely can be reconsidered!

Before delving further into the convoluted world of the motion to Reconsider, take a look at the rules guiding it:

❏ Cannot interrupt

❏ Requires a second

❏ Debate rules vary

❏ Isn't amendable

❏ Majority vote required

Several characteristics of this motion deserve mention. First, the motion to Reconsider can only be made by someone who voted on the prevailing/winning side. (The purpose of Reconsider isn't to allow the losers in a vote to keep bringing back an issue. It's to allow a motion to be revisited if someone on the winning side has changed their mind.) So, if a motion was adopted, reconsideration can only be moved by one who voted aye. If the motion was lost, the member must have voted no.

The first question from the chair following a motion to Reconsider is likely to be, "How did you vote on the motion?" If the vote was by ballot, you must be willing to reveal how you voted.

The requirement to have voted on the prevailing side leads to interesting voting scenarios. Depending on how a vote appears to be headed, members may vote opposite their position (or immediately change their vote) to be in a position to move to Reconsider. Otherwise, members might be forced to find someone on the opposite side who can be convinced to make the motion. (Such convoluted rules are a reason that some other parliamentary authorities have no restrictions on who can make the motion.)

The motion is also subject to time limits. In a typical meeting, the motion to Reconsider can only be made on the same day as the original vote. In a multiday convention, the motion can also be made on the next succeeding day of business.

Like the motion to Rescind/Amend Something Previously Adopted, there are situations in which the motion to Reconsider cannot be used. Such instances include:

- An affirmative vote whose provisions have been partly carried out
- An affirmative vote is similar to a contract in which the other party has been notified of the result
- A vote that has caused something to be done that cannot be undone
- A vote on the motion to Reconsider
- The original motion can still be renewed
- When the same result can be obtained by another parliamentary motion

The motion to Reconsider only requires a majority vote. That's because unlike Rescind or Discharge to a Committee, adoption of the motion to Reconsider doesn't resolve the issue. An affirmative vote on the motion to Reconsider simply brings the original proposal back to the floor for another vote.

The rules for the motion to Reconsider are different in committee (as if the motion wasn't confusing enough already). In a committee, the maker of the motion must not have voted on the losing side. That means a committee member who abstained or wasn't even at the meeting can make the motion. Also, there are no time limits on the motion to Reconsider in committee, so the motion can be made at any later date.

Incidental motions tend to deal with process and procedure. They have no order of precedence but arise during business and are resolved immediately. The most used Incidental Motions are Point of Order, Appeal, Suspend the Rules, Objection to the Consideration of a Question, Division of a Question, Division of the Assembly, Parliamentary Inquiry, and Request for Information.

Several motions don't fit anywhere else but serve to revisit an issue decided earlier. These motions include Take from the Table, Rescind or Amend Something Previously Adopted, Discharge a Committee, and Reconsider.

Chapter 7

Voting

Voting tends to be one of the most contested aspects of meetings. That makes sense because meetings are about making decisions. Whether or not an important resolution is adopted is based on the votes for and against it. Whether your candidate wins or loses is based on the votes for each nominee. And when votes or elections are close, it means the issue was contentious. As a result, votes often lead to controversy, disputes, and even lawsuits. In this chapter, I discuss various types of votes (elections are covered in Chapter 8). First, though, you should be aware of some basics of voting.

What Vote Is Required?

With any vote, a primary question is, "What vote is required?" Following is a rundown of the main bases for determining a voting result.

Majority vote. A majority is simply more than half. That could mean five votes in favor to one against. It could also mean 50.0001 percent in favor. Avoid the phrase *half plus one* because it can cause a vote to be announced incorrectly. See Chapters 5 and 6 to find out what kinds of motions require a majority vote.

Two-thirds vote. A motion requiring a two-thirds vote must receive at least two-thirds of the votes cast by members entitled to vote. Generally, any vote that restricts someone's right to participate (the motions to limit debate or to close debate) requires a two-thirds vote. Similarly, votes seeking to suspend a parliamentary rule usually require a two-thirds vote. People sometimes refer to a two-thirds vote as a "two-thirds majority vote." It's either a majority vote or a two-thirds vote, but not both!

Here's a simple rule for calculating a two-thirds vote without technology: Double the negative vote, and if the negative votes are more than the number of votes cast in favor, you don't have a two-thirds vote.

Plurality vote. A plurality vote simply means the proposal that gets the most votes, regardless of whether it is a majority. At times, elections of directors are by plurality vote because of state statutes or governing documents (see Chapter 8). You will also sometimes hear members suggest that a vote be by plurality when several options are available. It's true that such a vote is easy to calculate, but decisions by plurality are unlikely to represent the will of the members.

Robert's strongly recommends against plurality votes: "A plurality that is not a majority never chooses a proposition or elects anyone to office except by virtue of a special rule previously adopted."

How Is the Vote Calculated?

Votes are typically based on the number of members present and voting. If 100 members are present and the vote is 30 in favor and 20 opposed—and a majority vote is required—the motion passes, even though 50 members didn't vote! Members aren't required to vote; they can abstain. Abstentions are not counted for or against a proposal, and the chair should not call for abstentions during the vote. While statutes sometimes require elected officials on governmental bodies to vote, that's not the general parliamentary rule.

Instead of being based on those present and voting, a vote can sometimes be based on "those present" or on "the total membership of the board" because of the language in the rules or governing documents.

With such language, you have to be concerned with how many members are present at the time of the vote or the total membership.

Note: Such slight modifications in wording can make huge differences in the outcome of the vote. Also, abstentions matter with such language and will work against the motion. That's because every member who doesn't vote for the motion keeps it from reaching the threshold for passing, which is the same as a vote against the motion.

Let's suppose a meeting is dealing with a very important issue. The association has 200 total members. At this meeting, 100 members are in attendance. A vote is taken; there are 98 total votes, with 50 members voting in favor of the motion and 48 voting against it. Two members abstain. Depending on the basis of the vote, notice how the outcome varies dramatically despite the vote being the same:

A majority vote is	50
A majority of the members present is	51
A majority of the entire membership	101

What About a Tie Vote?

Members often ask about how to break a tie vote. In contrast to a tie during an election (see Chapter 8 for details), a tie vote on a motion isn't too much of an issue. If a motion requires a majority vote and only receives 50 percent of the votes, the motion fails because it didn't receive more than half of the votes. As to a two-thirds vote, the vote either is or isn't two-thirds, so the concept of a tie is irrelevant.

One additional issue regarding tie votes is more relevant to larger assemblies. As discussed in Chapter 1, the chair tends to be a full participant in smaller boards and votes on all issues. As a result, the chair's vote is already in the totals. That's not the case in larger assemblies where, except for a ballot vote, the chair tends not to vote unless his vote will affect the outcome.

That means the chair can impact the vote in one of two ways:

- **In the event of a tie:** The chair can vote *in favor* of the motion. Without that vote, the motion will fail, so the chair's vote will change the outcome so that the motion is adopted.

- **If a motion is going to pass by one vote:** The chair can vote *against* the motion. Because there is now a tie, the motion will fail.

The Most Common Methods of Voting

Of the many methods of voting, three approaches are used far more than all the others: voting by voice, rising, and show of hands. Because many meetings run into trouble in voting situations, you should pay close attention to how these votes are taken and the wording to use for each.

Voice Vote

The standard method of voting is by voice, particularly in larger organizations. *Robert's* even refers to voice voting as "the normal method of voting on a motion."

A voice vote should be taken by the chair as follows:

> "The question is on the adoption of the motion to [or 'that'] … [repeating or clearly identifying the motion]. Those in favor of the motion, say 'aye.' [PAUSE] Those opposed, say 'no.'"

> "The ayes have it, and the motion is adopted."

> [or]

> "The noes have it, and the motion is lost."

The correct pronunciation when asking for the affirmative vote is aye, like the "eye" in "eyeball." Also, while horses say "neigh," people say "no." When asking for the negative in a voice vote, the word is "no." (The word "nay" is limited to roll-call votes.)

As noted above, *Robert's* default voting method tends to be by voice unless a rule requires otherwise or the specific circumstances suggest another method is more appropriate. Motions requiring a two-thirds vote are an exception. Because a two-thirds vote can be difficult to hear, *Robert's* recommends a rising or show of hands vote for such motions.

Rising Vote

Large groups sometimes prefer to use an uncounted rising vote instead of a voice vote. That's particularly the case when taking a two-thirds vote, which can be easier to determine by seeing, rather than just hearing, the vote. The presiding officer can also verify a close voice vote with an uncounted rising vote (and as discussed in Chapter 6, the chair must take an uncounted rising vote following a voice or show of hands vote if a member demands a Division).

In any of these instances, the chair states:

> "Those in favor of the motion to invite Mr. Jones to be a guest speaker at our next meeting will rise. [Or 'stand.'] ... Be seated. ... Those opposed will rise. ... Be seated."

> "The affirmative has it, and the motion is adopted."

> [or]

> "The negative has it, and the motion is lost."

When a two-thirds vote is taken, the chair phrases the vote slightly differently:

> "Those in favor of the motion ... will rise. [Or 'stand'] ... Be seated. ... Those opposed will rise. ... Be seated."

> "There are two-thirds in the affirmative, and the motion is adopted."

> [or]

> "There are less than two-thirds in the affirmative, and the motion is lost."

If a count has been ordered by the chair or by the assembly through a motion and vote, the chair should put the specific numbers into the announcement:

> "Those in favor of the motion ... will rise and remain standing. [Or 'stand'] ... Be seated. ... Those opposed will rise and remain standing. ... Be seated."

> "There are 60 in the affirmative and 55 in the negative. The affirmative has it, and the motion is adopted."

> [or]

> "There are 55 in the affirmative and 60 in the negative. The negative has it, and the motion is lost."

A consideration with rising votes is to ensure that anyone who is unable to rise can still participate in the vote. Special rules often allow those who have difficulty standing to raise a card or express their vote another way.

Show of Hands Vote

In smaller organizations and boards, votes are most often done by a show of hands. The form for such a vote is similar to a rising vote:

> "The question is on the motion to purchase five copies of *Robert's Rules of Order Newly Revised*. Those in favor of the motion will raise the right hand. ... Lower hands. Those opposed will raise the right hand. ... Lower hands."

> "The affirmative has it, and the motion is adopted."

> [or]

> "The negative has it, and the motion is lost."

Except for the mention of raising and lowering hands, a show of hands vote mirrors the language for rising votes in instances of a two-thirds vote or a counted vote.

You might have noticed that all these voting methods have the presiding officer say exactly what members should do. "Raise the right hand." "Lower the right hand." "Rise." "Be seated."

Always use such clear instructions when voting. Vague language like "use the same sign" will lead to confusion. For instance, I've heard presiding officers ask for the "aye" vote and then ask for those opposed to use "the same sign." Some members said "aye," some who knew better said "no," and everyone was confused.

Other Methods of Voting

In some instances, the three methods of voting just described aren't the best techniques. That's especially the case if members carry different numbers of votes. For instance, delegates in conventions often carry the votes of members back home, which means different delegates have different numbers of votes. Shareholder votes might be weighted based on the number of shares owned. Condominium votes are often based on percentages of ownership. In such instances, voters carry different numbers of votes, so one member might have 1.05 votes and another 1.6 votes. To make matters more complicated, a member might also hold a "proxy" to vote on behalf of another member (discussed later in this chapter). In such instances, a voice or standing vote won't show the differences! Other methods of voting might be more appropriate in these situations.

Roll-Call Vote

A roll-call vote places each member on record as to his vote. Although time-consuming, a roll call can be used to ensure that weighted votes or proxies are accurately reflected. Unless there is a special rule controlling roll calls, such a vote can be demanded by a majority vote.

In a roll-call vote, the roll is called alphabetically, and each member may vote "aye" (or "yes" or "yea") or "no" (or "nay").

A member may also answer "present" (or "abstain") if they don't want to vote or "pass" if they aren't ready to vote but want to be called upon again. In roll-call voting, a record of how each member voted and the voting totals are entered in full in the minutes.

Machine or Electronic Vote at In-Person Meetings

Technology has replaced other methods of voting in some organizations. For instance, large association or union conventions might vote in elections or on important issues using machines similar to those used in political elections. Handheld electronic keypads are used in some meetings to quickly determine close votes. Cell phones can be used to text votes for instant tabulation.

Considerations before using any of these devices include the cost and learning curve involved. Advance notice and even demonstrations of the technology to members might be necessary for everything to run smoothly.

In today's ever changing world, you will sometimes hear the phrase "electronic voting" with regard to a vote taken with no meeting through online voting or an app. That's not the type of electronic voting mentioned here, which is focused on voting *during* an in-person meeting. Voting at virtual meetings will be discussed in Chapter 10, and voting electronically outside of meetings is a form of absentee voting (discussed later in this chapter).

Voting Card

A low-tech solution to weighted voting at in-person meetings can be large, brightly colored cardboard voters' cards or sticks. If this voting method is to be used, it should be authorized by a special rule of order. One advantage to voting cards is that they can be used to reflect multiple votes, so if a member is carrying several votes, the member can be given additional cards to reflect those votes. In such cases, a voting card vote will better reflect the vote than a voice or standing vote (because a person can't vote multiple times by voice or by standing).

When using voting cards, the vote is taken in a form similar to a show of hands vote:

> "The question is on the motion that the bill for building repairs be paid within 10 days. As many as are in favor of the motion, raise your card. ... Down. Those opposed, raise your card. ... Down."

Voting by Telephone

Sometimes, boards use voting by telephone in lieu of a physical meeting, but this must be authorized either by statute or the governing documents (see Chapter 10 on electronic meetings). Note that there's a huge distinction between an authorized telephone meeting and collecting the individual votes of board members by telephone.

Robert's states that the "personal approval of a proposed action obtained separately by telephone, by individual interviews, or in writing, even from every member of a board, is not the approval of the board, since the members lacked the opportunity to mutually debate and decide the matter as a deliberative body."

Ballot Vote

All the previously described voting methods are fairly open, but a ballot vote is typically used when secrecy is desired, such as in elections when people don't want others to know who they are voting for. Ballot voting is discussed with regards to elections in Chapter 8.

Ballot voting can also be used on issues when members have weighted votes, and a voice or standing vote might be inaccurate. In such cases, an organization can use a typical secret ballot or possibly a signed ballot (or *open ballot*). Such ballots are signed and are not secret. How is that useful? In weighted voting, it allows the organization to verify the members have not cast more than their allotted votes. In some organizations where members carry vastly different numbers of votes, all significant issues are voted on by ballot.

Absentee Voting

Most of *Robert's* is focused on decisions made in meetings. However, the book recognizes that statutes or governing documents might occasionally allow members who *aren't* at a meeting to participate. Such instances can include ballots permitted outside of a meeting or voting by mail, email or fax, or by proxy voting. Again, either the bylaws or state law must expressly allow such voting. *Robert's* tends to be of little help because such decision-making processes don't involve a meeting.

Voting by Mail

Voting by mail, email, or fax is generally reserved for when few members attend meetings, but a full membership vote is desired. Votes by mail are sometimes used by large national associations or large community associations. Some statutes even require certain types of votes, such as the election of directors, to be conducted by mail vote.

Before any vote by mail, detailed rules should be adopted as to the marking and returning of ballots. Very often, an inner envelope is sent to the voter with the ballot, in addition to a self-addressed, outer return envelope. That way, the vote of the member can be kept secret.

Preferential or Ranked-Choice Voting

Though beyond the scope of this book, preferential voting (or "ranked voting" or "ranked-choice voting") describes any number of voting methods by which the second or less-preferred choices of voters can be taken into account on a single written or electronic ballot. In other words, preferential voting is an attempt to allow repeated balloting with a single ballot. In one method, each voter ranks all candidates numerically. If no candidate wins among the first-choice votes, the votes for the candidate receiving the fewest first-choice votes are redistributed among the remaining candidates. This process continues until sufficient candidates receive the necessary votes.

There are numerous methods of preferential voting. Such varying methods tend to calculate and treat secondary choices differently, which can result in different outcomes.

Improper Straw Polls

Occasionally, a member will suggest taking an informal "straw poll" to test opinions on an issue. Beware! *Robert's* flat-out states that a straw poll "is not in order because it neither adopts nor rejects a measure and hence is meaningless and dilatory." It will also confuse the issue because members on the "winning" side of the straw poll won't understand why the results aren't binding on the assembly.

Proxies

A proxy is a power of attorney given to another to vote in the member's stead. In other words, if I give my proxy to Mary Smith, Mary can attend the meeting and participate on my behalf. But if Mary misses the meeting, it's as though I'm not at the meeting. My proxy only matters if Mary attends the meeting.

By statute, proxy voting is often permitted in for-profit and nonprofit corporations and community associations. Proxy voting is almost universally prohibited in board meetings because directors can't usually give away their responsibilities. Follow any statutory or governing document language as to proxies to the letter.

If proxies weren't complicated enough, there are five different generally recognized types of proxy:

- **General proxy:** The holder of the proxy has discretion to do whatever they want at the meeting.
- **Limited proxy:** The holder of the proxy can only vote on certain issues at the meeting.
- **Directed proxy:** The holder of the proxy can only vote as directed.

- **Limited directed proxy:** The holder of the proxy can only vote on certain issues as directed.

- **Quorum proxy:** The proxy only counts for purposes of obtaining a quorum and nothing else.

Without question, voting problems are sometimes caused by confusion between or a blending of different types of absentee voting. For instance, proxies mailed to members cannot be dropped off at the meeting like a ballot unless a person is named as a proxy and attends the meeting. *Robert's* specifically warns against adopting voting procedures where votes from those not at a meeting are combined with those in attendance. Unlike members at the meeting, those who have previously voted cannot adjust their votes to take into account debate, proposed amendments, or repeated balloting.

The vote required for a motion can vary based on governing documents and the parliamentary authority. A majority vote simply means more than half. A two-thirds vote is required for certain procedural motions and often to amend governing documents. There are numerous voting methods, including by voice, rising, a show of hands, roll call, and electronic devices at a meeting. The best voting method will be the one that is most appropriate for the specific group and motion under consideration.

Chapter 8

Officers and Elections

Selecting leaders is one of the most important responsibilities of an organization. Most often, this is done through a two-step process of recommending someone for office (*nominating*) and voting someone into office (*electing*). Because of the many disputes that arise from elections, it pays to handle the process properly.

In this chapter, I introduce you to the various types of officers and their duties. Of course, officers don't just appear out of thin air; they must be elected. To this end, I provide an overview of the various methods of nominating and electing individuals for office.

Officers and Their Duties

There is no fixed list of officers that all organizations must have. After all, a small assembly can survive with only a presiding officer and a secretary. In small organizations, the governing documents might even allow one person to hold more than one office. On the other hand, large associations might have a president, multiple vice presidents, a secretary and assistants, a treasurer and assistants, and more. If you want to know about the officers in an organization, check out the bylaws. Generally, though, you'll see at least the following officers.

President

President is the usual title for the presiding officer, but you see other terms depending on the specific organization, including *chairman*, *chairperson*, or *speaker*. (Such terms are not intended to designate male or female but are distinguished when addressing the presiding officer by "Mr. Chairman" or "Madam Chairman," as the case may be.) All these terms typically signify something more permanent than the designation *the chair*, which refers to the person presiding over the assembly at the moment. While this might be the president, it could also refer to a presiding vice president, or it might refer to an invited temporary presiding officer.

Bylaws generally provide many responsibilities for a president. A common duty is to preside over meetings, whether a membership meeting, board meeting, or recurring convention. It's not surprising that *Robert's* discussion of the president focuses greatly on running meetings. In fact, *Robert's* suggests that the presiding officer "should be chosen principally for the ability to preside." The ability to preside includes more than knowing parliamentary rules—personality, common sense, and tact all play a role. Even so, *Robert's* recommends that the president "make every effort to know more parliamentary procedure than other members."

In regards to meetings, a president has the following duties:

- Call the meeting to order once a quorum is present
- Proceed through the order of business
- Recognize members entitled to recognition
- Process motions that come before the body
- Enforce the rules of the assembly
- Respond to Parliamentary Inquiries or Requests for Information
- Declare the meeting adjourned in accordance with an adopted program or a vote of the assembly

If the president can't make a meeting, the bylaws should be clear as to who will preside. A similar issue occurs if the president relinquishes the chair to debate a motion.

In such instances (which should be rare), the president must vacate the chair and not return until the issue is resolved. The highest-ranking vice president would normally take over that proposal, but some bylaws give such responsibility to a president-elect.

If the president vacates the chair during a meeting and no vice president is available, the chair can appoint a chairman pro tem to temporarily preside. The situations I just described are a bit different than if the time for a meeting has arrived and no president or vice president is there. In that instance, the secretary or another member should call the meeting to order, and the assembly would then elect a chairman pro tem for the meeting.

Occasionally an issue comes along that is so complicated or the political situation so volatile that no one is willing to preside. In that case, a nonmember might be invited to preside over the meeting or issue. By a majority vote (but often unanimous consent), the assembly can ask a nonmember to preside so long as the president and vice president(s) don't object.

If either objects, an invited temporary presiding officer can still be utilized through a two-thirds vote to Suspend the Rules. Some parliamentarians regularly serve as professional presiding officers.

President-Elect

A president-elect is an elected officer who becomes president automatically the following term.

Not all organizations have a president-elect, and there are advantages and disadvantages to the position. A positive is that the president-elect can learn from the current president, be given certain duties, and prepare for their upcoming presidency.

A negative is that the organization is selecting a president far in advance and has little control if members change their minds.

To keep a president-elect from becoming president would actually require removing the president-elect from office. Also, for organizations where an existing officer ascends through vice president, president-elect, and president, the office can lengthen an already lengthy commitment.

Vice President

The vice president typically acts in the absence of the president. If the office of president becomes vacant, the vice president becomes president for the unexpired term. If there are several vice presidents, such as first vice president, second vice president, and so on, the highest-ranking vice president becomes president (and the other vice presidents usually move up). Only the largest organizations have multiple vice presidents.

The vice president might be anticipated to become the next president, but there is no automatic succession unless provided for in the bylaws—nor should there be. A vice president might turn out not to have the skills or personality to be a good president. According to *Robert's*, an organization "should have the freedom to make its own choice, and to elect the most promising candidate at that particular time" for president.

Secretary

Along with the president, the secretary is likely to be the most active officer. In fact, *Robert's* notes that a presiding officer and secretary are the "minimum essential officers for the conduct of business in any deliberative assembly." This office is sometimes called "clerk," "recording secretary," or "scribe."

Like other offices, the duties of the secretary should be clearly detailed in the bylaws. At a minimum, the secretary is responsible for the following duties:

- Keeping the minutes
- Keeping on file all committee reports

- Keeping the membership roll
- Making minutes and records available to members
- Signing copies of official acts
- Maintaining records, which includes the bylaws, special rules of order, other governing documents, and the minutes
- Giving notice of meetings to the members
- Assisting the president in preparing the order of business or agenda for each meeting
- Calling a meeting to order in the absence of the president and vice president to elect a chairman pro tem

Treasurer

Typically, the treasurer is the custodian of an organization's funds. The treasurer makes a full financial report annually and interim reports as needed. While the annual report should be forwarded to auditors for review, no action should be taken on monthly reports (see Chapter 11). The treasurer and all officers who handle funds should be bonded in an amount to protect the organization from loss.

Directors

Directors (the members of the board of directors or executive board) have such authority as given to them in the governing documents. Often, the directors are the highest governing body. For instance, in community associations the members generally elect the directors, who then run the association. In most national associations, the board of directors or executive board is the highest authority in the association when a convention or annual meeting is not in session.

Directors tend to be elected, appointed (often to fill a vacancy), or *ex officio*. An *ex officio* member of a board or committee is a member by virtue of another office or position held. For instance, a treasurer might be an *ex officio* member of the finance committee. If the *ex officio* member is a member or officer in the association, they have all the rights and responsibilities of other members. If the *ex officio* member is from outside the organization, the member has all the privileges of board membership but none of the obligations unless also serving as an officer.

Executive Director

The executive director (or executive secretary) is a paid staff person who manages the organization. Depending on the governing documents, this individual might answer to the board of directors or a smaller executive committee. Most often, the executive director is in charge of the headquarters office and staff. Despite being a salaried employee, the executive director is often made an *ex officio* member of the board in the bylaws. If so, the executive director is a full-fledged member of the board with the right to attend meetings, debate, make motions, and vote.

Parliamentarian

A parliamentarian advises the president and other officers, committees, and members on matters of parliamentary procedure. The operative word here is *advise*. The parliamentarian doesn't rule. That's the chair's job. *Robert's* is quite clear on who has the final say: "After the parliamentarian has expressed an opinion on a point, the chair has the duty to make the final ruling and, in doing so, has the right to follow the advice of the parliamentarian or to disregard it." The parliamentarian should be seated next to the presiding officer and discreetly call attention to any errors in the proceeding. Ideally, the parliamentarian should see what's about to happen and stop the error from ever occurring.

A parliamentarian must know more than just parliamentary motions. The effective parliamentarian should be familiar with the governing documents, including the bylaws, articles of incorporation, and any special rules of order.

In addition, the parliamentarian should be familiar with the adopted parliamentary authority for the organization.

To prepare, the parliamentarian should review the minutes or transcript of the prior convention or meeting. In addition, the parliamentarian should review any items noticed for the meeting, such as governing document amendments, resolutions, or new business items. Finally, the parliamentarian and president should discuss in advance any issues that might arise during the meeting.

A good parliamentarian has a number of responsibilities during the meeting. In addition to preventing parliamentary problems, the parliamentarian should keep track of the parliamentary situation. In large assemblies or conventions, that can include making a note of all motions and who has spoken. For greater detail, some parliamentarians keep a parliamentarian's log, which lists each motion, whether there was a second, who debated on each side, and the result of any votes. This information can assist the chair in assigning the floor to members to speak and resolve any confusion about the parliamentary situation.

It's easy enough to say a parliamentarian should warn the chair of potential procedural errors, but how exactly is that done? (After all, yelling *"DON'T DO IT!"* might not convey the right image.)

Different parliamentarians use different techniques. Some parliamentarians use a card system in which note-size cards have a brief description of parliamentary motions. These cards can be handed to the presiding officer, but they are most often clipped or attached to the lectern so that the president can view the parliamentary situation at any time. Such cards show both the motion before the body and the chair's wording for handling the motion. This method is professional, flexible, and inconspicuous. Other parliamentarians prefer scripts with complete language for all anticipated motions.

In virtual meetings, the parliamentarian might need to be physically present with the presiding officer during the meeting. Otherwise, some direct method of communication might be necessary.

In addition to assisting at meetings, parliamentarians can perform the following functions:

- Assist committee chairs with wording for reports and motions.
- Advise on bylaws and bylaws amendments.
- Help revise governing documents.
- Confer with the chair during breaks in order to anticipate upcoming problems.
- Assist or supervise with elections.
- Advise on presiding scripts.
- Advise on parliamentary tactics and strategy.
- Conduct training workshops for officers, board members, or leaders on running effective meetings.
- Provide formal parliamentary opinions.
- Serve as expert witnesses in court proceedings regarding meeting procedure.

Unless the parliamentarian is an attorney, the parliamentarian really shouldn't be interpreting procedural statutes or bylaws language. However, the parliamentarian should be aware of relevant laws and bylaws and bring them to the attention of the organization, which can then decide the meaning of the language or seek a legal opinion.

Smaller organizations might use a member as a parliamentarian, but this arrangement is less practical in a larger organization. A member parliamentarian has a duty to be impartial and doesn't make motions, debate, or vote (except in ballot votes). Even when abiding by these restrictions, a member parliamentarian might be viewed by some members as having a position or bias on issues. Or the parliamentarian might be associated with a certain group within the association. Because of these concerns, it is common in larger or more complex organizations to engage a professional parliamentarian (see Appendix A for a listing of professional parliamentary credentials and organizations).

Nominations

Prior to an election, it is common that the universe of potential candidates is narrowed down through nominations. A *nomination* is simply a proposal to fill the blank in the motion "that _____ be elected" with a name. Nominations are not actually required in a ballot vote because members are free to vote for anyone. However, without nominations to narrow the field, voting could go on for an extended period before a candidate achieves the necessary vote.

The most common methods of nominations are as follows:

Nominations from the floor. Under this method, once the chair asks for nominations, any member can suggest a name for election. Strictly speaking, a member doesn't need to be recognized by the chair to make a nomination. While no second is required for nominations, it's not unusual for members to second to show support for the nominee. After each nomination is made, the chair repeats the name for everyone to hear.

Generally, nominations from the floor remain open as long as anyone wishes to make a nomination. As soon as there are no further nominations, the chair declares nominations closed. If an official motion is needed, to close nominations requires an undebatable two-thirds vote. (Reopening nominations only requires a majority vote.)

Nominations by a committee. Bylaws sometimes provide for a nominating committee to recommend names for office. The advantage of a nominating committee is that the committee can consider the offices as a whole and take into account the skills necessary for certain positions. While the committee isn't limited to nominating one person for each position, doing so is a standard practice. After the nominating committee reports, the chair should ask for additional nominations from the floor (unless the bylaws have a filing deadline).

Unless the bylaws provide differently, members of the nominating committee can nominate themselves. Otherwise, the committee would be an ideal place to stick anyone the leaders don't want running for office!

Nominations by the chair. Depending on the bylaws, the chair may, at times, nominate individuals for various positions that require a vote of the members.

Nominations by ballot. While not as common, some organizations allow members to nominate through a process like election balloting. The nominating ballot never elects anyone to office; instead, it simply creates a list of nominees.

Nominations by mail. In large organizations with a scattered membership, nominations (as well as elections) are sometimes handled by mail vote.

Elections

After nominations are complete, the election is held. Bylaws often explain the process for elections. If the bylaws don't specify a process, the assembly can decide the method.

Before looking at the methods of election, I want to point out a couple of situations in which elections vary from other voting instances. For instance, elections most often require a majority vote. Unlike votes on motions, where a tie vote means the motion is defeated (see Chapter 7), a tie vote in an election means that the election is incomplete. In such situations, balloting is repeated as many times as necessary to obtain a majority vote for a candidate. *Robert's* has strong language about removing the lowest voting candidate from future ballots: "When repeated balloting for an office is necessary, individuals are never removed from candidacy on the next ballot unless they voluntarily withdraw—which they are not obligated to do. The candidate in lowest place may turn out to be a 'dark horse' on whom all factions may prefer to agree."

While majority vote is the default for elections, there are statutes governing for-profit and nonprofit corporations and community associations that provide that directors are elected by plurality vote. (That's right, whoever gets the most votes wins, even if it's three votes to two votes to two votes.) In Chapter 7, we discussed how a plurality vote never elects anyone to office without a specific rule. With elections of directors, you might find just such a rule.

Another process unique to elections is the concept of cumulative voting. In an election with *cumulative voting*, a member can cast one vote for each position to be filled. So, if three directors are to be elected, each member may cast three votes, which can be distributed among three individuals, or all three can be cast for one candidate. The concept behind cumulative voting is that it allows a minority group to secure the election of a board member. Cumulative voting is generally governed by state statutes and restricted to corporations.

Ballot Election

Ballot elections are common due to a desire to keep votes secret. However, keep in mind that sunshine laws generally prohibit ballot voting in governmental bodies. According to *Robert's*, if the bylaws provide for an election to be by ballot, that requirement is absolute. Here's the exact wording: "If the bylaws require the election of officers to be by ballot and there is only one nominee for an office, the ballot must nevertheless be taken for that office, unless the bylaws provide for an exception in such a case."

Ballots should be prepared in advance for distribution at the proper time, both to ensure accuracy and to make certain that only authorized ballots are in circulation.

If blank pieces of paper are used, different colors should be used to distinguish different ballotings. "Yes" and "no" or "for" and "against" boxes aren't used in elections. Instead, members should be instructed to mark or write a specific name (so that a voter can only vote against one candidate by voting for another or by writing in the name of another).

The language for a ballot vote in an election can be as follows:

Mark only one candidate for each office.

For President:

Alex Adams   _____

Betty Boop   _____

Chuck Capps   _____

_____   _____

Tellers appointed by the chair generally distribute, collect, and count ballots and report the vote. Tellers should be chosen for accuracy and dependability and shouldn't have a direct personal involvement in the election. Methods of folding ballots should be announced in advance or stated on the ballot.

A vote shouldn't be interrupted after any member has actually voted. An exception is when the ballots have been collected and other business is being transacted during the counting of the vote.

When balloting appears to have been completed, the chair should direct the tellers to collect the ballots by having members drop ballots into a receptacle passed by the tellers, drop their ballots into a central ballot box monitored by the tellers, or hand their ballots to a teller. When everyone appears to have voted, the chair declares the polls closed. If an official motion is needed, to close the polls requires an undebatable two-thirds vote. (Reopening the polls only requires a majority vote.) Generally, tellers count the ballots in another room.

When counting the ballots, irregular ballots might impact the outcome depending on the circumstances. Blank ballots should be ignored as scrap paper. Such blanks are not reported and don't affect the election in any way. In contrast, *Robert's* provides that "all ballots that indicate a preference—provided they have been cast by persons entitled to vote—are taken into account in determining the number of votes cast for purposes of computing the majority."

In other words, votes cast for Mickey Mouse or a ballot that is unintelligible are included in the total and could alter the outcome of the election. (Warning: Other parliamentary books ignore illegal ballots and could result in a different election outcome.)

When preparing the tellers' report, the tellers should list the total number of votes cast, the votes necessary for election, and then each person's votes from most votes to least as follows:

Tellers' Report

Office: President

Number of Votes Cast	100
Necessary for Election	51
Betty Boop received	55
Alex Adams received	20
Chuck Capps received	17
Ziggy Zappo (write-in) received	1
Illegal Votes	
Unidentifiable ballots	5
Mickey Mouse (fictional character)	2

The reporting teller never declares the result of a ballot vote, which is done by the chair. The chair's announcement should always include the actual vote count. Announcing the votes received by each candidate has procedural and political benefits. By hearing actual numbers, members might realize a counting or procedural error occurred in the balloting, which can then be corrected. In addition, candidates not elected might be less enthusiastic about challenging the results when they realize the vote spread was large.

The tellers' report is entered in full into the minutes. According to *Robert's:* "Under no circumstances should this be omitted in an election or in a vote on a critical motion out of a mistaken deference to the feelings of unsuccessful candidates or members of the losing side."

Voice Election

A voice (or viva voce) election is generally only appropriate when the bylaws don't require a ballot and the election isn't strongly contested. However, this method of voting is awkward.

Each candidate is voted on in the order they were nominated. That is, the chair states the person's name and says, "As many as are in favor of Mary Smith for president, say aye. ... Those opposed, say no. ..." As soon as any nominee receives a majority, that person is declared elected. If the noes are in the majority, the chair continues to the next nominee. You rarely see elections by voice because of the strangeness of voting each nominee up or down.

Election by Acclamation

A more common method of election is by unanimous consent or acclamation. This method is most appropriate when the bylaws don't require a ballot and only one person is nominated for an office (or just the right number of nominees have been made for open board seats). After ensuring that no one wishes to nominate someone else, the chair can simply declare the nominee elected by unanimous consent or acclamation. Most chairs, wanting to involve the members in the process, will ask, "Is there any objection to electing Sue Smith by acclamation? ... Hearing no objection, congratulations, Sue."

The specific officers in an organization and their duties should be outlined in the governing documents. At a minimum, most organizations need a president and a secretary. Nominations can aid the elections process by narrowing down the potential pool of nominees. While there are various options for elections, the best process will be the one that complies with the governing documents and is most appropriate for the circumstances.

Chapter 9

Types of Meetings and Quorum

If you've been paying attention, you've probably noticed that I use the word *meeting* throughout this book. In its strictest sense, a meeting is defined in *Robert's* as a single official gathering of members in one room to transact business during which there is no extended break, except perhaps for a short recess. For longer gatherings, you'll sometimes hear the word *session*. A session describes a series of connected meetings devoted to a single order of business, program, or agenda. In other words, a day or even the morning of a multiday convention might be considered a meeting. All days of the entire convention would be referred to as a session. The evening gathering of a society that meets every month would be both a meeting and a session.

There are several types of business meetings. These range from the usual meetings of the typical society to out-of-the-ordinary meetings called specifically to deal with a specific issue. This chapter examines the various types of meetings, how they're held, and what matters can be transacted at each. But first, let's look at a fundamental requirement that applies to all types of meetings—the issue of quorum.

Quorum

Quorum is the minimum number of members who must be present at a meeting to transact business. The quorum requirement protects the organization by preventing a very small number of members from taking action on behalf of the entire organization. Because of its importance, the quorum requirement applies to all types of meetings.

While there are a few exceptions for procedural motions, no business should be transacted unless there is a quorum.

Bylaws typically define the quorum for an organization, which can be an absolute number ("five members of the board") or a percentage ("20 percent of the votes in the condominium"). In the absence of bylaws language, *Robert's* establishes the following required quorums:

- For most organizations and boards, a quorum is a majority of all the members.

- In conventions, a quorum is a majority of those who have been registered as attending, which can vary greatly from the delegates appointed or elected.

- In mass meetings with no established membership, a quorum consists of those present at the meeting.

The perfect number for quorum varies by organization. A quorum that is too high might prevent the assembly from transacting business. A quorum that is too low might allow a small, unrepresentative group to act for the entire organization. According to *Robert's*, the quorum "should be as large a number of members as can reasonably be depended on to be present at any meeting, except in very bad weather or other exceptionally unfavorable conditions."

Be warned that statutes regularly tinker with quorums for nonprofits, governmental bodies, and homeowners and condominium associations. For instance, statutory quorums for nonprofit corporations and community association membership meetings are often quite low, such as 10 or 20 percent. At membership meetings, these same statutes regularly provide that once a quorum is present, it remains for the remainder of the meeting, regardless of how many members leave. Some states have provisions for homeowners associations that if a meeting doesn't have a quorum, it can reschedule the meeting for another date in which the quorum is halved (and the halving continues for each meeting until a quorum is met).

The prohibition on transacting business unless there is a quorum is a serious one. There seems to be an urban legend that business at meetings can continue without a quorum so long as no one raises the issue. Wrong! The general rule is that business transacted in the absence of a quorum is null and void. Members who vote on motions at meetings without a quorum can at times be held personally liable for their actions. Don't do it!

A few procedural steps can be taken in the absence of a quorum, including:

- Setting a continued meeting through the motion to Fix the Time to Which to Adjourn (see Chapter 5)
- Adjourning the meeting
- Recessing the meeting, in efforts to obtain a quorum
- Taking measures to obtain a quorum, such as rounding up members in the hall or contacting members

If some urgent matter can't be delayed and must be acted upon, the members proceed at their own risk with the hope that a later meeting with quorum will ratify the action (see Chapter 4).

While it might seem counterintuitive, a meeting without a quorum can still be called to order. At that point, however, the meeting must either adjourn or address one of the procedural motions allowed in the absence of a quorum. From a bylaws perspective, such a short meeting still counts as the organization holding its annual or monthly meeting.

So what happens if a meeting starts with a quorum but loses it during the meeting? Business must stop. (But again, there might be exceptions if a statute provides that a quorum at the beginning of the meeting remains, regardless of how many members have left.) The absence of a quorum is most often brought to the attention of the chair through a Point of Order or Parliamentary Inquiry ("Do we still have a quorum?"). Even if no one raises the issue, the chair has an obligation to make certain that a quorum is present at the meeting. At the point where it is realized there is no quorum, business (other than the procedural motions I point out earlier in this section) stops. A guest speaker or announcements might be allowed, but no further votes should be taken. In larger bodies, prior action is still valid because no one knows exactly when a quorum was lost. However, *Robert's* provides that when it can be shown that a quorum was missing for a prior vote by "clear and convincing proof" (such as the record of a roll call), even past actions can be challenged. Such a challenge would be raised through a Point of Order and subject to an Appeal (see Chapter 6).

Types of Meetings

There are many different kinds of meetings, including recurring regular meetings, special meetings to consider certain items of business or meetings to continue the work from a prior meeting. Such distinctions matter. The type of meeting can affect what notice is required to be given to the members, what business can be considered at the meeting, and even who may be present during the meeting.

Regular Meetings

A typical member of an organization might only be familiar with regular meetings. A regular meeting is the standard, recurring business assembly of a society or board. Depending on the governing documents, such meetings can be held weekly, monthly, or quarterly.

If the bylaws clearly state when regular meetings are to be held, no additional information may need to be sent to members. However, proper notice is one of the most important concepts in parliamentary procedure. That is, members have the right to know when meetings will be held. In fact, one of the quickest paths to trouble is to give inadequate or improper notice of a meeting. As a result, it's worth paying particular attention to the language in the bylaws regarding meeting notice. If, for instance, the bylaws provide that some number of days notice must be given of a meeting or convention, follow that language exactly. Without such notice, any business transacted at the meeting might be invalid. And unlike other meetings issues, notice problems can be quite difficult to fix. If a meeting requires 30 days' notice, and it is now 20 days to the meeting, there is no good solution other than to cancel and reschedule the meeting.

In *Robert's*, an important distinction arises based on how frequently an organization meets. Without getting too complicated here, *Robert's* spends considerable time discussing whether "no more than a quarterly time interval" has passed between regular meetings. The significance is because business items can be carried over from one session to another so long as there is no more than a quarterly time interval between meetings.

For instance, as noted during the discussion of the motion to Postpone in Chapter 5, an item can be postponed from one meeting to another so long as the next meeting is within a quarterly time interval. Similarly, an item laid on the table remains on the table until the end of the next business meeting so long as no more than a quarterly time interval has passed. Even an item of business not reached in the order of business can carry over to unfinished business at the next meeting so long as it is within a quarterly time interval (see Chapter 11).

As a consequence of this rule, *Robert's* does not allow a convention or annual meeting to postpone business to the following year. That's because business can only be postponed or delayed beyond a quarterly time interval by referral to a committee. The assembly could refer the matter to a committee to report back the following year.

Special Meetings

A special meeting (or *called meeting*) is a separate meeting of the organization held at a different time than regular meetings. Most importantly, a special meeting is called to consider one or more items specifically noticed in the call of the meeting. Without question, special meetings are another area where organizations can really screw things up. Improperly held special meetings are a regular area of meeting disputes and lawsuits.

The precise method of calling a special meeting should be provided for in the bylaws. This language explains who can call a special meeting, such as the president, the board of directors, or a certain number or percentage of members.

For nonprofit associations and community associations, state statutes often provide a means for members to demand a special meeting. Notice of a special meeting should include the time, place, and purpose of the meeting. That is, the subject matter of any business to be considered must be sent to members the required number of days in advance.

The importance of this notice is that it limits what can be done at the meeting. So if notice has been given that a special membership meeting will consider having an audit of the association's finances, members don't have to worry that the dues will be increased at the same meeting. Such a motion would be ruled out of order at the meeting as exceeding the scope of notice of the meeting. Even if such a motion were adopted, it would almost certainly be invalid.

While notice must be given of any business to be transacted at a special meeting, this rule is focused on substantive business items, not procedural ones. In other words, motions dealing with the conduct of the meeting are appropriate without notice.

Limits on debate could be established through a motion to Limit or Extend Limits of Debate. Discussion could be closed through a motion for the Previous Question. This makes sense in that unless procedural motions are permitted without notice, the members could never consider a motion to Adjourn!

Adjourned Meetings

An adjourned meeting is not the same as a meeting that has been adjourned. Instead, an adjourned meeting is a meeting that is a continuation of the current meeting. To avoid confusion of terms, other parliamentary authorities, such as *The Standard Code of Parliamentary Procedure*, refer to an adjourned meeting as a *continued meeting*.

An adjourned meeting most often exists because of some difficulty at the prior meeting. Perhaps there wasn't enough time to complete work on a specific motion at the prior meeting, so the meeting was adjourned to a different time and place. Or perhaps the quorum was lost during the meeting, so the meeting has been continued in hopes of getting a better turnout.

In either instance, the members would adopt a motion to Fix the Time to Which to Adjourn (see Chapter 5) to schedule a continuation of the current meeting. Except for reading and approving the minutes of the preceding meeting, an adjourned meeting picks up its work exactly where it was interrupted. *Robert's* does not require additional notice of the adjourned meeting to the members, as everyone at the meeting knows it was continued. But—and this is important—state statutes might require additional notice to members of the continued meeting.

Executive Sessions

An executive session (also known as a *closed session*) is a meeting (or a portion of a meeting) closed to all but members. That means that a board meeting could be closed to all but board members, and a membership meeting could be open to just members. Other individuals, such as the legal counsel or parliamentarian, can always be asked by the body to remain. (As noted in Chapter 8, *ex officio* members should also be included as members who have a right to be in a closed session.) The question of going into a closed session is usually handled by unanimous consent. The presiding officer simply asks, "Is there any objection to going into a closed session …?" If no one objects, the meeting is closed. If necessary, a motion can be made to go into an executive session, which requires a majority vote.

Members can be punished for violating the secrecy of a closed session. *Robert's* notes that nonmembers who attend are "honor-bound not to divulge anything that occurred."

It can be important to distinguish, though, between what was said in a closed session and what was done. Action taken in an executive session may be divulged to the extent necessary to carry it out. For example, if in a closed session, an officer is removed from office, it will be difficult not to disclose that action outside the meeting. The best practice is never to leave a closed session without an understanding of what is or is not secret.

There's a huge difference between how closed sessions are handled between governmental and nongovernmental bodies. As noted in Chapter 2, *sunshine laws* almost always prohibit governmental bodies from going into a closed session, except for a few specific purposes, such as discussing a legal issue with counsel. Even when a governmental body is allowed to go into executive session, typically, no action can be taken. That is, the body can only discuss the issue in a closed session, and any motions or votes must be made later in an open session.

In contrast, *Robert's* doesn't care whether your meetings are open or closed. There are no general parliamentary prohibitions on closed meetings or even rules for what can happen during the closed portion. *Robert's* allows both discussion and voting during an executive session. In fact, decisions made during a closed meeting don't even have to be revealed to nonmembers unless the assembly wishes!

While there is no all-inclusive list of what must be done in a closed session, the following matters are generally handled in closed session:

- Consulting with an attorney on legal issues
- Discussing litigation or prospective litigation
- Reviewing personal information that is confidential or should not be generally known
- Conferring about contracts or property purchases
- Reviewing employees or personnel issues
- Handling disciplinary matters

Minutes of an executive session (see Chapter 12) are only available to members who would have had the right to be in the closed session. In addition, the minutes of an executive session must be acted upon in a closed session.

Annual Meetings

In the parliamentary world, the term *annual meeting* has two different meanings. First, some organizations only hold one business meeting of the entire membership each year. For the rest of the year, an executive board runs the association. For instance, condominium and homeowners associations often only have one meeting of the members each year. This meeting, known as the annual meeting, elects the directors and conducts certain other business.

Another definition of an annual meeting is when the bylaws provide for one regular meeting where certain events occur each year. For instance, one board meeting of the several held each year might be known as the annual meeting and include reports of officers and committees, elections, and other specific business items.

Electronic Meetings

The world has changed so much in the last few years that electronic meetings and voting now require their own chapter (see Chapter 10).

Quorum is the minimum number of members who must be present to transact business at a meeting. Except for a few procedural motions, votes on motions should not occur without a quorum. Different types of meetings include regular meetings, special meetings, adjourned (or continued) meetings, executive session (or closed) meetings, and annual meetings.

Electronic Meetings and Voting

As evidence of how much the world has changed during the past decade (and especially in the last few years during the pandemic) with regard to transacting business, look no further than *Robert's* coverage of electronic meetings. The *11ᵗʰ Edition* of *Robert's* in 2000 devoted 3 pages and occasional references to making decisions electronically. The new *12ᵗʰ Edition* has significantly more, including 15 pages of "sample rules for electronic meetings." Virtual and hybrid (some members in person and some participating electronically) meetings are and will continue to be a part the meetings universe.

Authority Other Than *Robert's*

As discussed in Chapter 2, a higher authority such as state statute or governing documents can override the default provisions in *Robert's*. Some bylaws have express provisions for boards or members to meet by phone or virtually. During the pandemic, many states authorized temporary emergency orders allowing certain types of entities, such as for-profit and nonprofit corporations, to meet virtually so long as certain conditions were met. Many states have now enacted laws allowing those organizations and others to hold electronic board or membership meetings or for organizations to occasionally vote electronically with no meeting at all. Between advances in technology and changes in law, it's hard to keep up!

Please recognize that provisions in state law or higher documents are not *Robert's*. And this guide to procedure is mostly about *Robert's*. While I'll mention such laws and bylaws exist, it would be impractical to discuss if or how they apply to a specific organization (I'll leave that to the group's lawyer and parliamentarian). What this chapter provides is a general discussion of electronic meetings based on *Robert's*, as well as some guidance and tips on running better virtual meetings.

What Is an Electronic Meeting?

As a start, it's worth considering what is meant by "electronic" in the context of an "electronic meeting." After all, there are many different types of electronics: computers, phones, texts, faxes, augmented reality smart glasses, toasters, and more. As noted in Chapter 1, parliamentary procedure is mostly concerned with decisions made at *meetings*. *Robert's* gives its opinion of what a deliberative assembly is right on its very first page—a gathering of people "in a single room or area or under equivalent conditions of opportunity for simultaneous aural communication among all participants." In other words, the default in *Robert's* is that all members need to be able to talk to and to be heard by other members. (Without question, organizations with hearing or speech impaired members can also hold meetings, but special rules of order might be needed.)

In order to avoid confusion, *Robert's* also makes clear that a meeting does NOT include attempting to make decisions "in writing," whether by U.S. Mail, email, texting, or fax. Such methods simply don't meet the definition of a deliberative assembly. "When making decisions by such means, many situations unprecedented in parliamentary law will arise, and many of its rules and customs will not be applicable."

That means if you are trying to follow *Robert's* only, the term *electronic meeting*, by its definition, will be limited to audioconference (telephone or an audio-only platform) or videoconference (virtual technology that allows participants to both see and hear each other).

Requirements for Electronic Meetings

While the latest *Robert's* has far more language concerning the holding of electronic meetings than prior editions, that doesn't mean the book automatically allows them. Quite the opposite. *Robert's* provides that while an electronic platform that allows members to communicate with each other might meet the definition of a meeting, electronic meetings have to be authorized by express language in the bylaws. (But as noted earlier, state law might permit certain groups to meet virtually without an express bylaws provision.) Even if permitted by law, poorly worded bylaws can sometimes make it difficult to argue for virtual meetings. For instance, one set of bylaws had language that the annual membership meeting would be held "in alternating cities on the East and West coast." Such language was not only vague but was used to argue that only in-person meetings were permitted.

While talking about electronic meetings, it's worth noting that committees have slightly different rules when not meeting in person. Generally, committees can only meet virtually as follows:

- Committees established by the bylaws can hold electronic meetings only if authorized to do so in the bylaws.

- Special committees created for a specific purpose can meet electronically if authorized to do so by the parent body.

However, *Robert's* gives an additional option for committees in making decisions. "In the case of a committee, however, if it is impractical to bring its members together for a meeting, the report of the committee can contain what has been agreed to by every one of its members."

Rules for Electronic Meetings

It likely will be difficult to run a virtual meeting based only on language in *Robert's* or the bylaws. Special convention or meeting standing rules governing the virtual experience will almost certainly be necessary. That's because *Robert's* tends to focus on the in-person experience, and many of the normal recognition rules, such as standing or raising a hand, simply won't make sense. Similarly, normal convening rules often talk about what can or cannot be done "on the convention floor." Limits of debate that might seem appropriate for an in-person meeting might also seem far too long when watching the same person on a screen. Such temporary rules for a virtual experience tend to take the form of special rules of order (see Chapter 2).

As an example of what form such rules might take, the newest *Robert's* provides pages of "Sample Rules for Electronic Meetings" in an appendix. Generally, these sample rules are separated into four different types of potential electronic meetings:

1. Full-featured Internet or Internet/telephone meeting services with audio, possibly video, text, and voting

2. Teleconference with Internet voting and document sharing

3. Speakerphone to allow some members who are not physically present to participate in an otherwise in-person meeting

4. Telephone meeting without Internet support

Let's not get into the minutiae of all the possible individual electronic meeting rules, as those can be found in *Robert's*. Generally, however, the types of rules that should be considered for inclusion in such special rules of order include:

- Guidance on how members gain access to and participate in the electronic meeting, including the technology platform to be used by members for speaking and, if different, for voting.

- Specific items of business that will be considered.

- The steps a member must take to get recognized to speak or to make motions, such as whether motions are stated audibly or submitted electronically in writing.

- Members must remain muted when not speaking, and if they are speaking, members should reduce background noise as much as possible.

- Individual speaking limits, which will likely be shorter than at an in-person meeting. Normal debate limits in conventions of 5 or 10 minutes per member with up to two opportunities to debate tend to be far longer than members will tolerate online.

- Total debate limits on individual items, such as per proposal or resolution.

- All motions requiring a second are already deemed seconded. Waiting in virtual meetings for a member to be recognized, unmuting, solving technology issues, and identifying themselves just to say "second" takes up useful time in large virtual meetings.

- Certain motions will not be recognized or are out of order, depending on the specifics of the meeting. For instance, in a telephone meeting where motions cannot be seen by members, on-the-fly amendments from members might be unworkable. Other motions, such as to demand a rising vote, make little sense in a virtual setting.

- An individual connectivity issue is not a basis for a Point of Order or retaking a vote because one person having a Wi-Fi issue cannot be the basis for repeating everything.

For those who are just looking for a generic "good set of electronic meeting rules," there is no such thing. That's because the best rules for a specific meeting will vary based on the specific organization, its governing documents, the technology to be used for the meeting, and the issues and votes to be taken during the meeting.

Hybrid Meetings

The phrase "hybrid meeting" has no exact definition. Sometimes, it means an electronic meeting with separate physical gatherings of members for a single meeting. Most often, the term means a meeting at which some members are present in-person, and others participate electronically. For a small board of directors, such a practice might be common and not all that complicated. The simplest example would be a board meeting at which most members are in one room, and a member who is out of state participates by telephone conference call. Such an arrangement meets the "simultaneous aural communication" requirement of *Robert's*, and no additional rules might be necessary.

Contrast such a small board meeting to the concept of a "hybrid convention" with thousands of delegates. While it might seem that such an arrangement will be easier to arrange than an all in-person or all virtual gathering, that is not the case. Hybrid meeting arrangements and rules tend to be far more complex. After all, how do you make certain that members participating virtually are treated equally with regard to debating and voting as those in the room? Generally, as with absentee voting (see Chapter 7), it is difficult to combine votes in the room taken by voice or rising with electronic votes of those participating virtually. As a result, a system will likely be needed in which everyone votes electronically, even those present in-person at the meeting.

Differences Between In-Person and Electronic Meetings

Virtual meetings have many benefits. For instance, they can save significant travel time. Who wouldn't like to finish dinner at home and be online for a member meeting three minutes later? In addition, electronic meetings can allow members who might otherwise have work or family conflicts to participate virtually. A downside to virtual meetings is the learning curve and (possible) new costs associated with an online meeting or voting platform. Obviously, such concerns might not exist if a small board or membership meeting can meet through a straightforward online platform (such as Zoom or GoToMeeting or Microsoft Teams) to discuss and vote on issues just like at an in-person meeting.

For large deliberative bodies such as conventions and some annual member meetings, though, there are differences between in-person and electronic meetings. Such distinctions might lessen as technology improves and we become more familiar with online deliberation, but here are some examples of how virtual meetings differ from in-person meetings:

- Assume there will be some technology issue, whether big or small. I've been at in-person meetings where the power went out, and the meeting and voting continued uninterrupted through light from windows. Not so with electronic meetings. While electronic meeting technology keeps getting better, connection issues, outages, or coverage issues tend to occur that can impact virtual meetings significantly. At a recent large convention with excellent IT support, a software coding issue caused the online system to shut down when more than 500 members joined the meeting (which was a problem because there were several thousand delegates). The convention lost its first day of business. Regardless of how perfect the virtual platform might be, access to state-of-the art technology and connection speeds can vary significantly based on members' locations and resources. In other words, members might experience the same electronic meeting very differently.

- There is a different dynamic. While large in-person assemblies often fight over certain motions, there is still a feeling that it is a meeting of one organization. (Good presiding officers will sometimes reinforce the point by reminding delegates of what unites the members after particularly controversial votes.) Electronic meetings tend to feel like hundreds of individuals sitting somewhere else doing their own thing.

- There can be less transparency. At an in-person meeting, everything pretty much happens real-time. If a member feels that a rule has been violated, they head to a microphone to make a Point of Order. All other members or delegates can see what is happening. In a virtual meeting, most things happen behind the curtain. No one really knows who's "next in line" to speak, and a member might not be called on in the order they should be recognized (or at all). The temptation exists if a member is unruly to simply mute or disconnect them.

- There is generally less individual engagement. It's hard not to pay attention in a large physical meeting or convention. You aren't likely to fall asleep or have a telephone conversation when you are surrounded by others. There is no such buffer with virtual meetings. The fall-off between who is logged on for the meeting and who votes on proposals can be extreme. That's likely a function of what we all do while on virtual meetings— other work, surf the Internet, make a sandwich, complete other activities, and so on. In other words, members might only be attending the meeting with half (or less) of their eyes and ears. When delegates are not visible on a screen, it's likely even more common.

- Virtual meetings bring out the worst in some people. Members seem to be more willing to be mean and "in your face" than they would likely be in person. Virtual discussion is impersonal and, in some ways, similar to online chats and comments. People tend to be far more negative in such settings. At a convention, you have to go to a microphone and make your comments directly in front of hundreds of other delegates, often friends or peers. That dynamic likely causes members to be more circumspect. In contrast, individuals talking to screens from their living rooms tend to be willing to say most anything—no matter how ugly or confrontational.

- Virtual meetings can alter voting dynamics. Virtual votes can go differently than they would have gone in person. Most often, noncontroversial proposals tend to have more votes against them. Or there might be more votes to take controversial stands, remove board members or officers, or reject items that are usually easily approved each year. At an in-person meeting, you tend to vote by saying "aye" or "no" or rising in front of fellow members, often colleagues from your own organization. In other words, there are personality and group dynamics involved. You are also somewhat forced to be engaged in the process—you had to come to the meeting, and there is little to do during the proceedings but pay attention to the issues. In an online meeting, you are answerable to no one. You might also be paying less attention to the proceedings and voting with less information. Perhaps online voting gets closer to what members actually think, but you should recognize it is different.

- It's harder to "work out" things online. Controversial issues are often resolved on the floor or outside the meeting room at in-person meetings, possibly in hallways or after-hour events. For instance, maybe a motion to raise dues by "x" was going to fail, but members discussed the proposal and agreed to an adjusted figure. Being physically AT the meeting allowed that to happen. It is very difficult to work out differences during virtual meetings. Most proposals simply get an up or down vote as proposed.

- It is difficult to build a sense of community. There is more to meetings and conventions than simply voting on business items. Relationships get built. Friendships and trust are forged. All of that creates future leaders and builds a sense of community for the organization. Much of that happens elsewhere than on the floor, such as during social events or during conversations before or after meetings or during breaks. Future technology might get us there, but at present, it is difficult to build such relationships and a sense of community in virtual meetings.

Given the pandemic and new technologies, it has made sense to lean toward electronic meetings for the last couple of years. And now that we're familiar with the platforms, some hope we'll never go back to physical meetings. Virtual meetings have many positive benefits, and with time, might become very similar to in-person meetings. It's currently worth weighing the benefits and disadvantages of meeting in-person versus virtual meetings when deciding how to meet for a particular meeting or to decide a specific issue.

Tips for Better Virtual Meetings

As noted above, the technology and experience of virtual meetings keeps getting better and better. Even so, here are some thoughts and suggestions to improve any online meeting gathering to transact business.

Things take longer in a virtual meeting. Sometimes members can't be heard. Or the screen will freeze, and remarks have to be started over. Or the time to connect and recognize people isn't taken into account. However long you think a virtual meeting is going to take, assume it will take half again as much.

Someone should be assigned to troubleshoot any technology issues that might occur during the meeting, such as log-in issues, reconnecting dropped participants, helping people with speaker or microphone issues, or confirming that unknown phone numbers or electronic devices are delegates. It's hard to run the meeting as well as manage the technology.

Participants should be reminded to unmute themselves, either upon recognition or through an onscreen reminder slide.

Participants should be told to turn off their speakers. It is very distracting when a member speaks and those remarks echo back on their own speakers a few seconds later.

Unanimous or "general" consent (as discussed in Chapter 3) works well and can save time during in-person meetings, but not so much in large virtual meetings. Since members are likely muted, asking "Is there any objection to…," will likely be met with silence. Trying to use an online chat feature to have members type a response to the question tends to lead to confusion. As noted earlier, members seem more likely to object in a virtual environment than to yell out an objection at an in-person meeting. Given these difficulties in obtaining unanimous consent virtually, it might be faster to vote electronically on all issues, even noncontroversial ones.

Most online platforms have a "chat" or "text" feature that allows for communications between participants during the meeting. While that might be useful for other types of meetings, it can become a problem during an online business meeting if members begin to type their thoughts on the proposal being discussed. Debate is supposed to happen aurally on the floor. To allow a second "shadow" written debate leads to several problems:

- Such comments are unfair to members who are not participating virtually in a way that allows them to see the comments (such as by telephone only).

- Such comments do not fall under the normal debate rules as to how long and how many times members may "speak."

- Debate is supposed to be directed through the chair, who has little control over such texting.

- Online typed comments can become personal and not abide by the normal rules of debate etiquette.

As a result, if there is such a chat feature, meeting rules should restrict its use to items such as getting recognized to speak (if necessary) or IT problems. Substantive comments related to issues on the floor should be deemed out of order and possibly a basis for removal from the meeting, if egregious.

In a typical in-person meeting, the vote count on motions is not announced by the chair and not entered in the minutes. As noted in Chapter 3, votes on motions tend to be announced simply as having been "adopted" or "lost" (unless a count has been ordered or following a ballot vote). The nature of voting online pretty much requires that all votes be announced or shown as actual numbers or percentages. Because everyone knows that any electronic platform is tallying such results, if a full announcement is not made automatically, members will quickly ask for it.

Without higher authority such as state statute, *Robert's* requires clear language in the bylaws to allow electronic meetings. Even when permitted, *Robert's* provides that at a minimum, an "electronic meeting" must allow participants to talk and to be heard by the other participants. Electronic meetings can take various forms, ranging from full-featured online virtual meetings to everyone on speakerphone. It is likely that additional special rules of order will be needed for any meeting attempting to do business electronically, and the latest *Robert's* has sample rules. Regardless of how well the meeting goes, there are differences between in-person and electronic meetings that should be considered when arranging the meeting.

Chapter 11

Order of Business and Agendas

Have you ever noticed how different organizations often do things in a similar order during meetings? For instance, many organizations consider and adopt minutes somewhere near the beginning of the meeting. Have you ever seen minutes adopted as the *last* item of business? If not, that's probably because of the *standard order of business.*

The Standard Order of Business

The standard order of business is the customary order to the types of business that arise in meetings. From a meeting perspective, this order makes logical sense. It can also save you time.

Once the time to begin a meeting arrives and a quorum is present (see Chapter 9), the chair calls the meeting to order. The formal manner of doing this is for the chair to announce, "The meeting will come to order." At that moment, the meeting becomes official, and the members present can transact business on behalf of the entire organization. Rather than everything coming forward in a random hodgepodge, the standard order of business provides for the following groupings:

- Approval of the Minutes
- Reports of Officers, Boards, and Standing Committees
- Reports of Special Committees

- Unfinished Business
- New Business

(*Robert's* also includes headings for special orders and general orders. Consult the book if those are types of business your organization regularly considers because such items are beyond this book.)

The standard order of business makes sense within a meeting because it places categories of business in a logical order. After calling this meeting to order, the minutes of the previous meeting are taken care of. Then, you hear from officers or committees that have been working on matters for some time under "Reports." Then, you finish items of business that weren't finished at the last meeting under "Unfinished Business." Finally, you take up new items under "New Business."

While you might occasionally hear a chair use the phrase "the next order of business," that doesn't make sense from a parliamentary perspective. There's only one order of business, which makes up the entire meeting. A better phrase to use would be "the next item of business."

The following sections provide details on each item in the standard order of business.

Approval of the Minutes

In meetings where minutes are to be approved, such approval is typically done near the beginning of the meeting. Corrections to and approval of the minutes are typically done by unanimous consent. See Chapter 12 for details on minutes.

Reports of Officers, Boards, and Standing Committees

One of the first substantive items of business in a meeting is to hear from officers and established boards and committees. Such an arrangement is logical. Those who have been working on business for the organization should be given priority over new business items. While some chairs just go through the list of committee names each meeting, it makes much more sense for the chair to find out in advance who needs to report and only call on those officers, boards, and committees that have reports.

Reports can be presented for information only, in which case they don't require a motion or vote, or for action, in which case they require a motion and vote.

Many organizations assume that following any report, there must be a motion to Adopt the report. That's typically a mistake—and a bad idea. Let's say the Membership Committee has just reported that last week's new member reception had 1,000 attendees and cost $200. A member moves to Adopt the report. A vote follows, and surprise, the motion to Adopt the report is rejected. What have we just decided? Well, we have apparently decided that we didn't have a reception last month or that it didn't cost $200. There was no point in adopting this report because it was only to provide information. If a report is for information only, at the end, the presiding officer should simply say "thank you." Or the presiding officer could ask if there are any questions. The point is that when a report is solely for informational purposes, there should be no motion or vote.

A standard financial report is the best example of a report that should not be automatically adopted. Associations everywhere hear the treasurer give a financial report and then move to Adopt the treasurer's report. *Robert's* says you shouldn't do that. After all, we don't have the slightest idea if any of the bank amounts are accurate. Or even truthful. For all we know, our vote is the equivalent of "Yes, you're robbing us blind, but why don't we go ahead and approve whatever you just said." *Robert's* goes so far as to provide: "No action of acceptance by the assembly is required—or proper—on a financial report of the treasurer unless it is of sufficient importance, as an annual report, to be referred to auditors." The *auditors' report* is what should later be adopted by the body.

In *Robert's*, an auditors' report doesn't necessarily mean a full-blown audit by a certified public accountant. It could be that, but it also could be a lesser compilation or review, or simply a careful review of the organization's finances by a committee of members (called an *auditing committee)* or by elected officers referred to as *trustees.*

You'll know if a report is intended for action because of the wording at the end of the report. For instance, a committee tasked with recommending the location for the next convention might report something like this: "Madam Chair, our committee investigated three cities as potential convention sites. We loved one city, didn't like another, and never actually found the third. *On behalf of the committee, I move that next year's convention be held in Raccoon City.*" See the difference? You know this report is for action because it ends with a motion. We aren't going to vote on the entire report, just the motion at the end. As you'll recall, motions from committees already carry a second, so the chair would simply state: "It is moved and seconded that next year's convention be held in Raccoon City."

In conventions and some other organizations, you'll hear a slightly different type of committee report. When members are permitted to submit resolutions or proposed bylaws amendments for consideration, a committee will occasionally review the proposal. Such committees range from ones that do nothing other than recommend that a member proposal be adopted or rejected to ones that can completely rewrite the proposals. Because these committees are reviewing someone else's proposal, they will often end with a recommendation rather than a motion. In other words, "The Resolutions Committee has reviewed Resolution number 8, feels it is the best thing since sliced bread, and recommends that the resolution be adopted." In such organizations, the proposal is generally already before the body and does not need to be moved or seconded again. As a result, the chair simply moves forward with, "The committee recommends that Resolution number 8 be adopted. Is there any discussion on the resolution?"

You'll occasionally hear a member incorrectly move to "receive" a committee report. If you've just heard the report, it's already received! To receive and to adopt a committee report are two very different things.

Reports of Special Committees

Reports of special committees are pretty much the same as reports of standing committees. The only difference is that standing committees exist because they are mentioned in the bylaws and have a continuing existence, while special committees are created to perform a specific task. For example, a special committee might be created to plan the retirement celebration of the executive director. Because of their transitory nature, special committees rank slightly below standing committees in the standard order of business.

Unfinished Business

Let me unequivocally state that there is no category of business known as "Old Business." As in the chair incorrectly asking, "Is there any old business?" Business that carries over from the previous meeting is properly known as "Unfinished Business." The problem with the term *old business* is that it sounds like this is the part of the meeting where we can talk about any "old" thing we've ever discussed in the history of the organization. That's a very bad idea. In contrast, *unfinished business* makes clear these business items have carried over from the prior meeting. We must deal with such motions at this meeting because they weren't "finished."

For organizations that meet at least quarterly, unfinished business typically falls into one of three categories:

1. Any matter that was on the previous meeting's agenda but didn't get reached

2. Any matter that was being discussed at the previous meeting when the meeting adjourned

3. Any matter that was being discussed at the previous meeting that was postponed to the current meeting

The chair never needs to ask if there is any unfinished business because the chair should know what did or didn't get finished at the prior meeting. As a result, the presiding officer simply states the question on the first item of unfinished business. Or, if there is no unfinished business, the chair can skip this category altogether or simply announce that there is no unfinished business.

New Business

Typically, most work in a meeting is accomplished when dealing with new business. In this agenda category, members can introduce new items for consideration. Unless there is a rule or a statute to the contrary, anyone can propose most anything. That obviously can make planning a meeting quite difficult, so some organizations have notice requirements in their bylaws or through a special rule of order to require business items be submitted in advance. Governmental bodies subject to sunshine laws, such as school boards and city councils, almost always require motions to be submitted days before the meeting due to open meetings laws. Such a requirement makes sense for most organizations because it helps when preparing the agenda and avoids last-minute surprises.

In an organization without advance-notice requirements, the presiding officer introduces the category by simply asking, "Is there any new business?" Members can then introduce a motion by being recognized, making the motion, and getting a second (f seconds are necessary—see Chapter 3). Following the consideration of each item of business, the chair repeatedly asks, "Is there any further new business?" This process continues until there are no additional business items (or members tire of new business and move to Adjourn).

Notice how the standard order of business helps you move business *between* meetings. If you decide to adjourn the meeting and haven't finished all items, that's fine. The three new business items that you didn't reach move up in the next meeting to unfinished business. In this way, the standard order of business "percolates" new business items and filters them to the top.

Closing the Meeting

In most assemblies, the chair can adjourn the meeting without waiting for a motion to Adjourn. Once all items of business have been considered, the chair can ask, "Is there any further business?" If no one responds, the chair can state, "Since there is no further business, the meeting is adjourned."

If custom or tradition requires that a motion to Adjourn be made, the presiding officer can ask, "Is there a motion to Adjourn?" Once the motion is made and seconded, the presiding officer can ask, "Is there any objection to adjourning the meeting? [PAUSE] Hearing no objection, the meeting is adjourned." As with other instances of unanimous consent, if anyone objects, the chair can process the motion formally.

In addition to these basic provisions of the standard order of business, there can be others. Common ones include Opening Ceremonies, Announcements, or the Program. Some unions and other assemblies include a Good of the Order, where members can offer informal observations on the organization without the need for a motion.

The Consent Calendar

A recent trend, especially among governmental bodies, is to include a category of business known as the *Consent Calendar*, *Consent Agenda*, or *Unanimous Consent Agenda*. The purpose of this category, which is often near the beginning of the meeting, is to handle all noncontroversial items at one time.

For instance, a Consent Calendar heading might be placed in the order of business near the beginning of the meeting and include on it the approval of the minutes. Other routine, administrative matters that are approved at each meeting might also be included. When you reach that category on the agenda, the chair would state, "You will see four items on the Consent Agenda: A, B, C, and D. Is there any objection to approving all items on the Consent Agenda?" If there is no objection, all four items on the Consent Agenda are approved together.

On the other hand, if a member wishes to discuss or objects to one item, the chair would state: "Item C is objected to. Is there any objection to approving the other items on the Consent Agenda: A, B, and D? Hearing no objection, A, B, and D are approved. Item C will be considered later in the meeting." Like any motion for unanimous consent, the purpose of a Consent Calendar is to quickly move through noncontroversial items so that there will be more time for controversial items.

Agenda

Although based on the standard order of business, an agenda is an even more valuable tool for keeping meetings on track. After all, the standard order of business is still just a general outline for the meeting. That is, reports or new business are kinds of business and don't really give you the specific items that will arise at the meeting.

If you really want to manage your meeting, you need an agenda. With an agenda, the specific items that are expected to come up at a meeting are placed into the order of business. That is, the three unfinished items from last month are listed under "Unfinished Business." The two new motions that you know will be introduced are placed under "New Business." And so on.

There is no better use of a presiding officer's time than preparing a good agenda. With that said, it's important to realize that there are several types of agendas.

The Informal Agenda

A typical agenda lists all items in the order they are expected to occur. For instance, an agenda might look like this:

Agenda

[Call to Order]

Consent Calendar

      a. Minutes of March 12 Meeting

Reports

      a. Government Relations Committee

      b. Legal Counsel Update
        (in Executive Session)

Adjourn

Such an agenda is simply handed out before or at the beginning of the meeting. No vote is taken on it. As a result, the agenda is really just a general guide to items that are expected to be handled at the meeting. How does this help? Because you expect members to behave differently if they know there are 2 versus 15 business items. The purpose of an informal agenda is simply to give everyone an idea of how much work is before the group. The downside to such an agenda is that it is not binding.

The Adopted Agenda

The assembly can also adopt an agenda, either through a motion and vote or through unanimous consent. This is frequently done near the beginning of the meeting, often in the Consent Agenda. By adopting the agenda, the assembly "locks in" both the items of business as well as their order. Now, if a member wants to change the order of items or introduce a new item, he must ask the body to change the agenda. Adopted agendas are particularly useful in conventions or annual meetings where members don't have much time and don't need surprises. (See Chapter 9.)

Once a majority vote adopts an agenda, it can be changed by a two-thirds vote to Suspend the Rules. Or a motion to Postpone a specific item can be made when the question arises, in which case you would then move to the next item in the agenda.

The Timed Agenda

The timed agenda is a more recent trend. While the timed agenda originally seemed more common to church governing bodies, you see it at all sorts of meetings now. This type of agenda looks similar to the earlier informal agenda, but a time is listed next to each item.

Timed Agenda

7:00	[Call to Order]
7:01	Consent Calendar
	a. Minutes of March 12 Meeting
7:02	Reports
7:02	a. Government Relations Committee
7:30	b. Legal Counsel Update (in Executive Session)

8:30	Adjourn

As to each item, the chair (or chair and staff) has estimated how long each item on the agenda will take. Does this sound like a lot of work? Absolutely. But it might be worth the effort. After all, how can a chair know how long a meeting will take if no thought has been given to the length of items on the agenda? To prepare a timed agenda, the chair typically starts with the end time of the meeting and works backward, giving more time to some items and less to others. Like the informal agenda, the timed agenda is simply a suggested guide. Without question, it speeds the meeting along. About five minutes after an item on a timed agenda was supposed to start, you can see members start to look at their watches! Still, like the informal agenda, a timed agenda isn't binding.

The Adopted Timed Agenda

You knew where this was headed! For groups in need of serious intervention, an adopted timed agenda might be the answer. Once adopted, not only is the order of items locked in but so are the actual times. For instance, at 7:30 p.m., the chair would say something like: "It's now 7:30. We decided as a group by a vote that at 7:30, we would move into the legal counsel update. Unless someone wishes to make a motion to change the agenda, we will now begin the legal counsel update."

Why would a group subject itself to such a rigid schedule? Well, there are two obvious reasons. Some organizations simply can't rein in the length of their meetings, and an adopted timed agenda might help. A second use of an adopted timed agenda is when there is limited time for several important items. Let's say that an organization has two hours to consider two important motions. Human nature is that the group will spend most of the time on the first matter and then hurriedly deal with the second matter in the last few minutes. With an adopted timed agenda, the organization can guarantee one hour for each motion.

The standard order of business places categories of business in a logical order and includes approval of minutes, reports, unfinished business, and new business. An agenda expands on the order of business by listing specific business items in order. A good agenda is worth the effort!

Chapter 12

Meeting Minutes

Much of this book is focused on what happens during a meeting. At times, though, the question involves how to prove what happened at an earlier meeting. Was a bylaws amendment approved or rejected? What was the final wording of an adopted resolution? Minutes can help resolve such issues because once approved, they are the official record of actions taken.

Most often, the governing documents of an organization prescribe that the secretary is responsible for taking and maintaining minutes of meetings. Even without such language, *Robert's* gives the secretary the duty of keeping the minutes and committee reports and making such documents available to the members. Without further direction in the governing documents or state statute, this means that general members are entitled to the minutes of membership meetings, board members are entitled to the minutes of board meetings, and so on. It's also important to note that minutes prepared by the secretary are nothing more than draft minutes until approved by the assembly, most often at the following meeting.

Well-written minutes are invaluable. Members who were absent might want to know what occurred at the meeting. In the event of a dispute, minutes are the best proof of whether a proposal was adopted or the exact wording of a motion. Minutes have even resolved lawsuits over what happened at a meeting, sometimes decades after the original decision. Taken together, the minutes can be the best history for an organization.

A Minute on Minutes

Minutes should be kept for all meetings of boards, conventions, and regular meetings of an organized society. Although many committees also keep minutes, *Robert's* is not quite so demanding, noting only that a "brief memorandum in the nature of minutes" be kept for the use of the committee. Legislative bodies also keep minutes, but they are usually more detailed and referred to as the *journal*. With any organization that maintains minutes, the minutes are often grouped for some period of time—such as a year or decade—in a book or binder called the *minutes book*. Past minutes should also be scanned or backed up on a computer for protection.

From a parliamentary perspective, the overriding theme of minutes is that they are a record of what was *done* at a meeting, not what was said. Consequently, if your minutes use the word *said* while describing debate, they have too much information. According to *Robert's*, minutes are a record of action taken at a meeting, not what was said by members or guests. There is no need to frantically summarize debate. Once a meeting ends, we really don't care what members said. We don't even need to know how each member felt about a specific motion. What we need is the exact wording of each proposal and whether it was adopted or rejected. Without question, some organizations want more detailed minutes, including summaries of debate. For instance, many conventions keep much greater information in a large document known as the *convention proceedings*. Some assemblies even keep a word-for-word transcription of everything said. If that's something you want, so that in retirement you can reexperience every moment of every meeting, knock yourself out. Just recognize that those really aren't minutes; they are a verbatim transcript. Minutes are a short, to-the-point account of business transacted so that readers can quickly determine what was done.

Some secretaries like to record meetings to help in preparing the minutes. And in today's world, there is sometimes an electronic recording of an entire online virtual meeting. Neither the recording nor a transcription of it can take the place of minutes. A common practice is to destroy such recordings after the minutes have been prepared to avoid confusion about the "official" record.

Chapter 2 noted higher authority that can override usual parliamentary practices. If your organization is governed by statute and you only follow the language in *Robert's*, your minutes might be wrong! Some boards must keep more detailed minutes because of state law. For instance, governmental bodies, including school boards and city councils, might have to keep debate summaries or even a listing of how every member voted on each issue. Such statutes might also provide who has access to particular minutes and for how long.

What You Should Put in the Minutes

If you want to follow *Robert's*, minutes generally include only the following. The first paragraph states:

- The type of meeting—regular, special, or adjourned (see Chapter 9)
- The name of the organization
- The date and time of the meeting
- The location of the meeting, particularly if the location varies
- Whether the chair and secretary were present, or the name of the individuals who substituted for them
- Whether the minutes of the previous meeting were read and approved

Next, you should include a separate paragraph for each of the following items, providing:

- All main motions, including the wording and disposition of each main motion, as well as any amendments
- All motions that bring a main question again before the assembly, including the wording and disposition of the motion
- Any procedural motions necessary to avoid confusion (such as a motion to Suspend the Rules that allowed a motion to be introduced that would not normally be permitted under the rules)
- All notices of motions
- All Points of Order or Appeals, whether sustained or lost

The final paragraph is the shortest and easiest. It simply states the time of adjournment.

Several other standard practices for minutes include:

- Recording the names of makers of motions
- Giving the exact vote in the event of a counted vote or a ballot vote
- Minutes used to be signed "Respectfully submitted," but that is no longer necessary. Standard practice now is to simply have the minutes signed by the secretary.

Can an organization include other information in its minutes? Absolutely! Each organization can decide for itself what the minutes should contain. As an example, *Robert's* doesn't mention listing the names of those attending a meeting in the minutes. But many groups, especially small boards, list everyone present (and sometimes even those absent).

What You Shouldn't Put in the Minutes

Typically, minutes do not include:

- Any debate or discussion on motions.

- The names of seconders. (As noted in Chapter 3, after a motion has been discussed or a vote has been taken, the lack of a second just doesn't matter.)

- Remarks of guest speakers.

- Motions that were withdrawn. (This is the case unless the motion needs to be mentioned for the minutes to make sense, such as if the sole motion to be considered at a special meeting is withdrawn.)

- How specific members voted on a motion based solely on the secretary looking around the room (a roll call is required to place on the record how each member votes; see Chapter 7).

- Personal opinions on anything said or done. (While this might seem obvious, I've seen minutes where the secretary commented on a member having the "bad sense" to introduce a particular motion.)

Using the standard format, minutes tend to be pretty short. Look at the following minutes from a two-hour meeting, which might fit on a single page!

Bright High School PTA

November 6, 2022, Regular Meeting

The regular monthly meeting of the Bright High School PTA was held on Tuesday, November 6, 2022, at 7 P.M., at Bright High School, the Chairman and the Secretary being present. The minutes of the October meeting were read and approved as corrected.

The report of the Treasurer was received and placed on file following questions to the Treasurer.

The motion relating to the year-end teacher appreciation event, which was postponed from the October meeting, was then taken up. On motion of Marty Smith, the motion was referred to a committee of three to be appointed by the chair with instructions to report at the next meeting.

Pam Rogers moved "that the Board participate in a leadership retreat to be held the second weekend of February." After amendment and further debate, the motion was adopted as follows: "That the Board participate in a leadership retreat to be held on two consecutive weekends beginning the first weekend in June."

The meeting adjourned at 8:50 P.M.

Fred Jones, Secretary

Approving the Minutes

Draft minutes become official minutes by being voted on by the body. However, many organizations spend far too much time considering and approving minutes. You're going to read the minutes out loud? Wake me when you're done. The second comma should be replaced with a semicolon? Just shoot me! When handled properly, approving minutes should take less than a minute.

There's little reason why draft minutes can't be sent to all members in advance—if not by mail, then electronically. At a minimum, the proposed minutes should be at every member's place at the beginning of the meeting. This version should be clearly marked as a draft so they aren't confused with the final adopted minutes. At the appropriate time in the agenda (see Chapter 11), the chair should ask if there are any corrections to the minutes. Any corrections tend to be handled "without objection." If none, or once any corrections are dealt with, the chair can use unanimous consent to ask, "Is there any objection to approving the minutes?" If there is no objection, the chair declares the minutes approved.

Of course, when the chair asks if there are any corrections to the minutes, there might be some. Any suggestions can be resolved, preferably also by unanimous consent. If any proposed changes are significant or controversial, they should be handled through a formal motion to Amend (see Chapter 5). If members wish to actually discuss the minutes (which should be a rare occurrence), debate and a formal vote can be used. In most instances, however, unanimous consent can be used to quickly and painlessly approve the minutes.

The latest *Robert's* recommends a slightly different process for approving minutes (while also noting that a motion to approve the minutes is not out of order). Once any corrections are handled, the *12th Edition* provides that the chair can simply declare the minutes approved. The thought seems to be that since corrections have been resolved, no vote is actually necessary to approve the minutes. While *Robert's* allows this practice, members are far less likely to be confused about whether the minutes have been approved if they are involved in the process.

For organizations that don't meet often, such as the annual meeting of a condominium association or a national convention, waiting a year or more to resolve the minutes doesn't make much sense. Because of that, groups that meet once a year typically don't approve minutes. This makes sense in that members are unlikely to recall what happened a year earlier. In fact, the voting body might be composed of completely different members. For such groups, the more common practice is that the executive board or a committee (called the *Minutes Approval Committee*) is authorized to approve the minutes shortly after the meeting. While the entire organization can always revisit the minutes the following year, this process allows the organization to have official minutes without waiting 12 months.

Once adopted, the draft minutes should be changed to ensure they are approved and official. Different approaches include removing the word *draft*, the secretary signing the official minutes, or adding a date of approval to the minutes.

While some members believe that actions adopted at a meeting aren't final until the minutes are approved at the next meeting, that's not true. The minutes aren't what make an adopted motion valid, but are simply a record of what happened at the meeting.

Changing Minutes After the Fact

Are minutes ever wrong? Of course! And sometimes the error isn't noticed until long after the minutes have been approved. No problem. Like most motions adopted by an assembly, you can revisit a motion to approve the minutes through the motion to Amend Something Previously Adopted (see Chapter 6). With proper notice, a majority vote (or a two-thirds vote with no notice) can modify approved minutes—even years later.

Recognize that there is a huge difference between correcting the minutes and changing the underlying action. If a set of minutes lists board members in attendance, and John wasn't at last quarter's board meeting, the adopted minutes can be corrected to reflect that. But if John *was* at the meeting, we can't alter reality by simply removing his name from the minutes.

Similarly, one group adopted a motion to send six delegates to a national convention but later changed its mind. So, the body simply amended the minutes to remove any mention of the motion. While that removed any record that the motion had been adopted, it didn't do anything to change the motion itself! The proper course of action would have been to Rescind (see Chapter 6) the motion to send six delegates to the national convention. The minutes of the current meeting would reflect that the motion to Rescind was adopted, and the earlier motion was no longer in effect.

As succinctly stated in *Cannon's Concise Guide to Rules of Order*: "Think of the minutes as a report on the weather at the last meeting: you cannot change what the weather did on that day. Nor can you change what the members did; you can correct only a misstatement as to what actually happened."

Minutes of Executive Sessions

As discussed in Chapter 9, an executive session is a meeting or part of a meeting that is closed to nonmembers. The purpose, of course, is so that nonmembers won't hear what's going on. So what should be done about the minutes? After all, if nonmembers can read all about the executive session in the minutes, it defeats the purpose of closing the meeting. This problem is solved by keeping separate minutes of executive sessions.

Depending on the circumstances, minutes of an executive session might not have much in them. Some groups go into closed session simply to discuss a concern, such as evaluating an employee or talking about an issue. In fact, most governmental boards (such as school boards and city councils) are prohibited from doing anything in closed session but talk (see Chapter 9). Due to state statute or their governing documents, some homeowners and condominium associations have similar restrictions. Since minutes are a record of what was *done* at a meeting and not a record of what was *said*, there would be no minutes of an executive session consisting only of discussion. The minutes would simply show the body went into closed session and then later came out.

On the other hand, if action is taken during a closed session, the minutes of the executive session should reflect that. The problem, of course, is that anyone hearing or seeing the minutes will know what happened during the "secret" portion. That's why minutes of an executive session aren't read or acted on in open session. Instead, the executive session minutes are only available to those who had the right to be in the closed session unless the body decides otherwise. At the next meeting, the body must go back into closed session to review and approve the minutes from the executive session.

Executive session minutes are usually kept separate from the standard minutes, or at least kept in a sealed envelope that says "Executive Session Minutes." Only members who had a right to be in the executive session have access to such minutes. That is, board members have access to board executive session minutes. Association members have access to executive session minutes of general membership meetings. If the reason for secrecy no longer applies, the group can always vote to open up the minutes. For instance, if the purpose of a closed session was to decide on the bid price for a piece of property, the minutes no longer need to be kept secret after the property has been purchased.

Minutes Template

Minutes are fairly formulaic. That is, for a specific organization, the minutes will look pretty similar from meeting to meeting. As a result, you can prepare a template in advance that you can use to record the minutes.

While a minutes template will look different for each organization, here's an example:

Minutes Template

MINUTES OF [ORGANIZATION]

[DATE]

The _____ [regular, special, adjourned] meeting of the _____ [organization] was held on _____ [day of week, date, time] at the _____ [location], with President _____ [name] presiding and _____ [name] as secretary.

[Some boards and small organizations tend to list those who are present or absent.]

Members attending:

Members absent:

Minutes: The minutes of the [date] meeting were approved [or "approved as corrected"]

Officers' reports:

     President

     Vice President

     Secretary

     Treasurer

Board and committee reports:

Unfinished business:

Motion: _____ [Name] moved that _____ [state motion]

MOTION CARRIED OR MOTION FAILED (select one)

New business:

Motion: _____ [Name] moved that _____ [state motion]

MOTION CARRIED OR MOTION FAILED (select one)

Announcements:

The meeting adjourned at _____ [time].

_____

[name], Secretary

_____

Date of approval

Skeletal Minutes

Why wait until the meeting to prepare the minutes? If you're considering a template for meetings, go all the way. Write the minutes *before* the meeting! Well, maybe not completely, but *skeletal minutes* (or *mock minutes*) can get you most of the way there. Having much of the minutes done before a meeting even starts is often easier and less stressful than pulling everything together after a long, tiring meeting.

Like a minutes template, skeletal minutes are prepared before a meeting. The difference is that skeletal minutes include the specific items you anticipate coming up at the meeting. With a good agenda and a notice requirement for motions, you should have a pretty good idea of what particular proposals will be discussed. Similarly, for a convention, you might know weeks in advance of every resolution or bylaws amendment that will be presented. You just don't know which motions will eventually be adopted, defeated, or amended.

With skeletal minutes, you fill out all information in the minutes, including when the meeting is, where it is, who may attend, and the actual wording of motions or items to be considered. During the meeting, you simply note what happens to each motion and add any additional items that arise unexpectedly. I have seen secretaries use this technique to complete the minutes of a convention that considered 300 resolutions within minutes of the end of the meeting. Sure beats starting the minutes after the meeting!

The official record of what happened at a meeting is the minutes. Good minutes reflect what was *done* at the meeting, not what was said by members. Both the correction of and approval of minutes tend to be done by unanimous consent. If necessary, minutes can always be corrected after the fact. Minutes templates and skeletal minutes are techniques for preparing much of the minutes in advance of a meeting.

Chapter 13

Solving Meeting Problems

When you get right down to it, this entire book is about solving meeting problems. Good governing documents and proper parliamentary procedure prevent many issues from ever becoming problems. Even so, a few remaining concerns can derail a meeting. For instance, what do you do in the event of a problem member (or, for that matter, a problem chair)? Wouldn't it be nice to avoid these and other problems altogether? In this chapter, I offer up proven tips for keeping meetings on track.

The Problem Member

The term *problem member* covers a host of sins—everything from someone being intentionally disruptive to members who are well-meaning but still annoying and who negatively impact meetings.

Take the situation where a member is too participatory, whether because of personality or feeling passionate about a particular issue. Aspects of formal procedure can help equalize participation, including the rule that no one may speak a second time while there are members who want to speak a first time and the rule that no one may speak more than twice to a motion.

However, what if yours is a small board that follows less-formal procedure? Even in informal settings, the chair can encourage new discussion—and prevent repetition—by asking specifically for speakers who have not yet spoken. And whether a group is large or small, the chair always has some responsibility to act as a traffic cop. That is, if a member tries to jump in for a second or third time while others wish to speak, the chair (like an officer in an intersection) might need to hold out a hand palm-forward to "stop" the member and say, "Charlie, you've already spoken twice. Let's hear from Mary."

The reverse of too much involvement is a member who simply won't participate. This can be caused by a variety of reasons, whether apprehension or simply an unwillingness to fight for recognition against more aggressive members.

In small boards and committees, the effect of one or two members not speaking can be as detrimental as a member speaking too much. Certainly, not everyone needs to give input on every issue. However, in a smaller body, if the chair notices that a member appears to want to say something but isn't speaking up, there's nothing wrong with the chair acting as a therapist. "Susan, you haven't said anything on this important issue. Is there anything you'd like to share?" The best-case scenario is that you get a new viewpoint. The worst-case scenario is that Susan says, "No, thank you." (If such a direct question might cause undue stress, the chair can approach the member in advance during a break.)

Another style of problem member is one who constantly brings up new ideas or topics during discussions of something else. Such suggestions might be intended to be helpful or even valuable but they are off point to the issue under discussion. Such digressions must be controlled, or a meeting will go off track. A good presiding officer will acknowledge that a tangential issue has been raised, but note that it isn't relevant to the discussion and should be taken up later.

Some small boards or committees use a flipchart or whiteboard to "park" off-topic discussions for another time. (Some even refer to it as the "parking lot.") That allows the issue to be recognized and addressed later without interrupting the current discussion.

A different type of meeting disruption is when two members enter into a direct conversation or argument. Such situations often begin with a question to a member that escalates. Once again, the formal procedure is designed to prevent this circumstance by requiring all remarks to be addressed to the chair. That includes questions to a member speaking in debate. If it appears that members are starting a back-and-forth discussion, the presiding officer should remind everyone to address all comments to the chair.

The issues discussed so far are more related to personality; however, there are individuals who intentionally or unintentionally become a disruption at meetings.

As a starting point, *Robert's* distinguishes between procedural actions that can be taken with a disruptive member versus a disruptive guest.

A nonmember is a guest and, if disruptive, may be removed by order of the chair acting alone. (Obviously, the assembly could arrive at a different position through a Point of Order or an Appeal.)

While the chair might have such a right, it generally isn't wise to physically remove anyone from a meeting. In today's world, the possibility of violence or a lawsuit is just too great. Instead, every possible step should be taken to defuse the situation. Such efforts might include any of the following actions:

- Taking a recess to allow things to calm down
- Taking a recess and speaking with the individual
- Taking a recess and having others speak with the individual
- Creating an adjourned meeting (see Chapter 5) and continuing the discussion at another time
- Simply adjourning the meeting altogether

If a situation arises at an in-person meeting where someone must be physically removed from a meeting, you should call on the assistance of official security or law enforcement personnel.

Unlike guests, members typically have the right to attend meetings pursuant to governing document language. As a result, many more steps—and even the assembly's involvement—are required to remove a disruptive member. *Robert's* provides several levels of response depending on the severity of the offense:

- For a minor offense, such as saying something inappropriate or referring to another member by name during debate, the chair can lightly rap the gavel once and admonish the member to avoid repeating the mistake in the future.

- For a more serious offense, the chair can warn the member or call him to order by stating, "The member is out of order and will be seated." In such a situation, the member is not permitted to continue speaking until the issue is decided by the body. The question is put to the assembly in the undebatable motion, "Shall the member be allowed to continue speaking?"

- For the most serious offense, the chair can "name" the member. This can lead to the imposition of a penalty by the body as a whole, which might include the following: requiring an apology, censuring the member, requiring the member to leave the current meeting, or suspending or expelling the member from membership. *Robert's* has many protections for both the assembly and the member, so it's best to review the language in *Robert's* in such a situation.

Unlike violations occurring in a meeting that are resolved immediately, member violations outside of a meeting generally require an investigation and trial. The distinction is that members weren't present to witness the offensive act. Flip to the last chapter of *Robert's* for details on the disciplinary process.

The Problem Chair

Past editions of *Robert's* mostly limited the discussion of how to control a chair with the motions Point of Order and Appeal (see Chapter 6). That is, a member who believes the chair has made an inadvertent or intentional procedural error can raise a Point of Order, which demands a ruling. Depending on the chair's ruling, any member and a seconder can Appeal the decision of the chair to the body for decision.

In what might be a sign of the times, more recent *Robert's* have significantly more discussion on handling an out-of-control presiding officer. If the chair refuses to rule on a properly made (and not dilatory) Point of Order, the member should again attempt to obtain action by the chair.

If the chair still ignores the member, the member can stand in place, address the body, and put the Point of Order to a vote. That is, the member states, "Is the Point of Order that … well taken?"

Robert's notes that if the Point of Order was the result of the chair ignoring a different properly made and seconded motion, the member puts that motion (instead of the Point of Order) to a vote without debate.

The language regarding an ignored Appeal is similar. If the chair ignores an Appeal that has been properly made and seconded, the member can stand and put the Appeal to a vote without debate as follows: "Shall the decision of the chair be sustained?" Without question, *Robert's* is clear that a member putting a motion to a vote is a last step only taken after several attempts to get the presiding officer to do the right thing. However, there must be a means for moving the business forward even if the chair is derelict in their duty.

Also, *Robert's* now describes removing a presiding officer from chairing all or part of a session. The process varies depending on whether the person presiding is a temporary presiding officer or the regular chair.

- **For a temporary appointed or elected chair:** A motion can simply be adopted to "declare the chair vacant and proceed to elect a new chair." Such a motion is an incidental main motion (see Chapter 4) and requires a majority vote.

- **If the offending presiding officer is the regular chair:** A motion to Suspend the Rules can be adopted by a two-thirds vote to remove the chair's authority to preside during all or part of the meeting. If such a motion is made and seconded, the chair must be turned over to the next highest-ranking vice president to process the motion. In the absence of any vice presidents, a chairman pro tem should be selected to preside over the motion.

A motion that suspends the chair's authority to preside only applies to the current session and has no impact on any administrative duties of the chair outside of a meeting. To permanently remove the presiding officer requires that the bylaws language on removal be followed. In the absence of such bylaws language, the *Robert's* process can vary, depending on whether the word *and* or *or* appears at a specific location in your bylaws (see *Robert's* section 62 if you're intrigued).

Meeting Problems Resolved

Now that we've discussed problem members and problem chairs, let's consider how to avoid many meeting problems altogether. Without question, a good meeting plan leads to a better meeting. That's because what happens before the opening gavel strikes can be as important as what happens during the meeting. Indeed, the success of some meetings is determined long before the call to order. With that in mind, consider each of the following questions before your next meeting:

Why meet? Some groups meet because statutes or governing documents require so many meetings per year. Except in such instances, the best reasons for a group meeting are for decision making, problem-solving, planning, and evaluation. If the purpose of a meeting is just to give information, there might be easier and cheaper ways to accomplish that, such as an email or webinar.

What are the desired outcomes? There's a difference between discussing an issue and adopting an issue. Any meeting plan should reflect the difference. For example, suppose the desired outcome for a condominium meeting is to adopt a special assessment. In that case, the meeting should be arranged so that there is a specific proposal to adopt the assessment, followed by a discussion and vote.

Who is responsible for each item on the agenda? Too often, meetings are simply left to chance, or the presiding officer just handles everything. Meetings run more smoothly, are more inclusive, and will be more productive if other members have responsibilities. Arrange in advance for various members to have certain duties, whether giving a report, making a motion, or participating in introductory ceremonies. Attendance will be better if members have a role in the agenda. More importantly, members are likely to feel part of the organization if they do more than sit and listen.

Have you confirmed the setting? A bad environment can cause a meeting to fail as quickly as a poorly planned meeting. Rooms that are too large or small, hot, cold, or noisy can affect participation.

Test all equipment, including microphones and projectors, to make sure nothing will likely fail at an inopportune moment. Even a room's layout can drastically alter the atmosphere. Auditorium-style seating usually leads to less participation by members. On the other hand, an oval or circular arrangement invites discussion to the point where it can be difficult to make members stop talking.

A compromise often used for smaller meetings is a horseshoe pattern, with the presiding officer in the middle opposite the open side. This layout encourages participation but acknowledges that the chair is leading the meeting.

Have you created an effective agenda (or at least followed the standard order of business)? There's nothing more important to a successful meeting than a well-planned agenda. Such an agenda should have a start and end time for the meeting. Depending on the number of items and type of meeting, you might want to indicate a start and end time for each item. (See Chapter 10 for details.)

Should notice of business be required in advance? Some governmental bodies and some governing documents require that business items be submitted in advance. Without question, it helps planning the meeting to know if there will be one or ten main motions to discuss. Also, allowing substantive business to be brought up on the fly can lead to poorly worded motions.

Typically, organizations that require business to be submitted in advance can still get around the rule for urgent matters. For instance, a motion to Suspend the Rules would permit a main motion to be introduced despite a special rule requiring notice of motions. However, statutes requiring advance notice of motions for governmental bodies or special meetings generally cannot be suspended.

Because meetings are fluid and each situation is different, there is no perfect list of suggestions for all meetings. However, here are some tips that will work for most organizations to run a smooth, productive meeting that members appreciate. The following suggestions are appropriate whether a meeting is procedurally formal or informal:

- **Start the meeting on time.** Reward those who are on time, not those who were tardy.

- **Stick to the agenda.** Don't allow off-the-cuff issues to distract you from what you came to do. You might want to consider an adopted agenda; timed agenda; or an adopted timed agenda (see Chapter 11).

- **Have an endpoint in mind.** Keep the meeting moving so that you can adjourn when you reach the end time.

- **Preempt debate.** Resolve noncontroversial items through unanimous consent. Or have a consent agenda near the start of the meeting that includes all noncontroversial items.

- **Manage discussion.** Encourage new discussion and prevent repetition by asking for speakers who have not spoken. If a matter is likely to be lengthy, consider setting total debate time.

- **Alternate pro and con.** After hearing from a proponent, ask if there is anyone who wishes to speak against the motion. If no one wishes to speak on a particular side, it might be time to ask for unanimous consent to end debate. If discussion appears to have reached diminishing returns, the chair can always ask for a motion to close debate.

- **Encourage and equalize participation.** Make sure no one monopolizes the discussion.

- **Use informal procedures when practical.** A meeting does not need to be more formal, parliamentary-wise, than necessary.

- **Control interruptions and digressions.** When possible, even announcements should be held until the end to avoid disruptions to the flow of business.

- **Manage conflict.** The chair should intervene whenever it appears that members are getting into a back-and-forth discussion or addressing each other disrespectfully.

Always keep in mind that the chair sets the tone for the meeting. Yes, that's a huge responsibility. *Cannon's Concise Guide to Rules of Order* states it well: "If the Chair is an effective leader—focusing on the members, treating each fairly, earning everyone's trust—then the meeting will be successful."

Several instances where the chair "got it" come to mind.

One association elected an aggressive advocate as president in a hotly contested election. About half the members and most observers assumed a miserable year lay ahead. Instead, the new president treated members fairly, went out of his way to be respectful to all (including the opposition), and ran efficient meetings. When asked about his behavior change, the president explained that as a member, his job was to advocate; but as president, his role was to preside over the assembly fairly.

In another situation, two different school boards faced a similar divisive issue. In each, the members argued for months on how to handle the difficult situation. At the meeting of the final vote, the two chairs handled the process quite differently. In one, the chair said he'd heard all he could take and that he was putting the issue to an immediate vote. Upon announcing the result, he said something like, "Thank heavens that's over. Meeting adjourned!"

The second board chair expressed that she understood the difficulty of the decision and that members were voting how they felt best, but that for the sake of the board and its constituency, she hoped that everyone, regardless of the vote, would come together to work toward their common purpose. Upon announcing the vote, the chair wished everyone a good evening and that she looked forward to seeing everyone at the next meeting, ready to work on new issues.

The members of the first board hardly spoke to each other for several meetings because the toxic atmosphere. In contrast, the members of the second board had started coming back together by the following meeting and were functioning as a board by the next. The difference? The second chair understood that her role was to set the tone.

Finally, end the meeting on a positive note. With the many alternatives these days to attending meetings, volunteers cannot be thanked too often. Acknowledging and sincerely thanking members for their time is not only gracious but likely will result in greater enthusiasm for the organization. And that, in turn, will lead to even better meetings.

Meeting problems can take a variety of forms. Problem members can include those who try to participate too much, as well as those who will not participate. A good presiding officer can take steps to address both extremes. Disruptive members must be dealt with immediately by the chair. When presiding officers do not properly perform their duties, members can take several procedural steps. Anyone responsible for arranging or running a meeting should give thought to every aspect that could impact the meeting's effectiveness.

Parliamentary Resources

I hope this book has inspired you to delve deeper into the fascinating world of meeting procedure. If so—or if you have additional questions—here are some excellent parliamentary resources in the form of organizations, books, and websites.

Parliamentary Organizations

Three national organizations deserve mention. The National Association of Parliamentarians and the American Institute of Parliamentarians certify parliamentarians as well as provide parliamentary procedure programs and publications. The American College of Parliamentary Lawyers is a forum for lawyers with parliamentary credentials.

National Association of Parliamentarians (NAP)

The National Association of Parliamentarians was founded in 1930 and is the oldest and largest parliamentary organization. It publishes the quarterly journal *National Parliamentarian*, which contains educational articles on parliamentary procedure and articles on NAP activities and chapters.

NAP membership classifications include Members (Regular and Honorary) and Credentialed Members (Registered Parliamentarian [RP], Professional Registered Parliamentarian [PRP], and Retired Credentialed Parliamentarian). There is an examination requirement for NAP membership based upon the latest edition of *Robert's*.

For more information:

National Association of Parliamentarians
888-NAP-2929
www.parliamentarians.org

American Institute of Parliamentarians (AIP)

The American Institute of Parliamentarians was founded in 1958. A traditional distinction between NAP and AIP has been a greater emphasis in AIP on authorities beyond *Robert's*.

AIP might be best known for its parliamentary practicums, which are multiday programs offering education in parliamentary procedure, including lectures, workshops, and group projects.

AIP's quarterly *Parliamentary Journal* contains educational articles on parliamentary procedure. AIP publishes a separate newsletter with articles on the activities of AIP and its chapters.

AIP membership classifications include Individual (Regular, Certified Parliamentarian [CP], Certified Professional Parliamentarian [CPP], Retired, and Full-Time Student) and Associate (for associations, institutions, or corporations). There is no examination requirement for AIP membership.

For more information:

American Institute of Parliamentarians
888-664-0428
www.aipparl.org

American College of Parliamentary Lawyers (ACPL)

The American College of Parliamentary Lawyers was founded in 2007 to acknowledge attorneys who have distinguished themselves in the practice of parliamentary law, provide a forum for the exchange of information among experienced legal professionals, and offer educational opportunities for members and nonmembers to discuss, advance, and improve the public's knowledge of parliamentary law. To be eligible for membership in the college, an attorney must be credentialed within NAP or AIP and have contributed to the parliamentary profession through teaching and writings.

For more information:

American College of Parliamentary Lawyers
www.parliamentarylawyers.org

Books About Parliamentary Procedure

Anyone studying parliamentary procedure should own (and preferably have opened) the official, latest *Robert's*, which is *Robert's Rules of Order Newly Revised (12th Edition)*.

In addition, the following books will either make *Robert's* more understandable or offer alternatives to some of *Robert's* practices:

> *Notes and Comments on Robert's Rules (Fifth Edition)*, by Jim Slaughter (with original author Jon Ericson).

I'm biased, of course, but this is an excellent resource written in an easy-to-follow question-and-answer format that makes *Robert's* approachable. The book provides commentary and comparisons with other parliamentary authorities, especially in the notes, and addresses the procedures of larger assemblies and conventions.

> *Robert's Rules of Order Newly Revised in Brief (Third Edition)*, by Henry M. Robert III, Daniel H. Honemann, Thomas J. Balch, Daniel E. Seabold, and Shmuel Gerber.

An introduction to the latest *Robert's* by the *Robert's* authors.

> *The Standard Code of Parliamentary Procedure (Fourth Edition, Revised by the AIP).*

Originally by Alice Sturgis, *The Standard Code* has for decades served as a shorter, simpler alternative to *Robert's*.

> *American Institute of Parliamentarians Standard Code of Parliamentary Procedure.*

While not a direct successor to *The Standard Code*, this is a newer work based on the principles of Sturgis.

> *Demeter's Manual of Parliamentary Law and Procedure*, by George Demeter.

While out of print, *Demeter's Manual* is an excellent source to use when double-checking an answer to complicated problems.

Parliamentary Websites

www.aipparl.org
American Institute of Parliamentarians

www.jimslaughter.com
My website, which includes many charts and articles on meeting procedure, parliamentary news updates, and links to numerous parliamentary resources

www.lawfirmcarolinas.com
Blog articles on *Robert's* and meeting procedure from my law firm, Law Firm Carolinas.

www.parliamentarians.org
National Association of Parliamentarians

www.parliamentarylawyers.org
American College of Parliamentary Lawyers

www.robertsrules.com
Official *Robert's Rules of Order* website

www.groups.io/g/Parliamentary/topics
Online discussion of parliamentary law and procedure, including various parliamentary authorities

www.sites.google.com/site/enapunit Electronic Unit of the National Association of Parliamentarians (eNAP)

Parliamentary Motions Guide

Note: A full-sized copy of this chart can be printed or downloaded for free at www.jimslaughter.com.

Parliamentary Motions Guide

Based on *Robert's Rules of Order Newly Revised (12th Edition)*

The motions below are listed in order of precedence. Any motion can be introduced if it is higher on the chart than the pending motion.

	YOU WANT TO:	YOU SAY:	INTERRUPT?	2ND?	DEBATE?	AMEND?	VOTE?
§21	Close meeting	"I move to **adjourn.**"	No	Yes	No	No	Majority
§20	Take break	"I move to **recess for …** "	No	Yes	No	Yes	Majority
§19	Register complaint	"I rise to a **question of privilege.** "	Yes	No	No	No	None
§17	Lay aside temporarily	"I move to **lay** the question **on the table.** "	No	Yes	No	No	Majority
§16	Close debate	"I move the **previous question.** "	No	Yes	No	No	2/3
§15	**Limit or extend debate**	"I move that debate be limited to …"	No	Yes	No	Yes	2/3
§14	**Postpone to a certain time**	"I move to postpone the motion to … "	No	Yes	No	Yes	Majority
§13	**Refer** to committee	"I move to refer the motion to … "	No	Yes	Yes	Yes	Majority
§12	Modify wording of motion	"I move to **amend** the motion by … "	No	Yes	Yes	Yes	Majority
§11	Kill main motion	"I move that the motion be **postponed indefinitely.** "	No	Yes	Yes	No	Majority
§10	Bring business before assembly (a **main motion**)	"I move that … " [or] "I move to … "	No	Yes	Yes	Yes	Majority

Jim Slaughter, Certified Professional Parliamentarian-Teacher & Professional Registered Parliamentarian
336-378-1899 (W)   336-378-1850 (F)   P.O. Box 41027, Greensboro 27404   website: **www.jimslaughter.com**

Side 1

Parliamentary Motions Guide
Based on *Robert's Rules of Order Newly Revised (12th Edition)*

Incidental Motions: No order of precedence. Arise incidentally and decided immediately.

	YOU WANT TO:	YOU SAY:	INTERRUPT?	2ND?	DEBATE?	AMEND?	VOTE?
§23	Enforce rules	**"Point of Order!"**	Yes	No	No	No	None
§24	Submit matter to assembly	**"I appeal** from the decision of the chair."	Yes	Yes	Varies	No	Majority
§25	Suspend rules	**"I move to suspend the rules** which …"	No	Yes	No	No	2/3
§26	Avoid main motion altogether	**"I object to the consideration** of the question."	Yes	No	No	No	2/3
§27	Divide motion	**"I move to divide the question."**	No	Yes	No	Yes	Majority
§29	Demand rising vote	**"I call for a division."**	Yes	No	No	No	None
§33	Parliamentary law question	**"Parliamentary inquiry."**	Yes (if urgent)	No	No	No	None
§33	Request information	**"Request for information."**	Yes (if urgent)	No	No	No	None

Motions That Bring a Question Again Before the Assembly: No order of precedence. Introduce only when nothing else pending.

§34	Take matter from table	**"I move to take from the table** …"	No	Yes	No	No	Majority
§35	Cancel or change previous action	**"I move to rescind** …" [or] **"I move to amend something previously adopted** …"	No	Yes	Yes	Yes	2/3 or maj. w/ notice
§37	Reconsider motion	**"I move to reconsider the** vote …"	No	Yes	Varies	No	Majority

Jim Slaughter, Certified Professional Parliamentarian-Teacher & Professional Registered Parliamentarian
336-378-1899 (W)   336-378-1850 (F)   P.O. Box 41027, Greensboro 27404   website: **www.jimslaughter.com**

Side 2

Index

N

O